TWENTY-FIRST CENTURY MILITARY
HELICOPTERS

TODAY'S FIGHTING GUNSHIPS

TWENTY-FIRST CENTURY MILITARY
HELICOPTERS

TODAY'S FIGHTING GUNSHIPS

Steve Crawford

MBI

This edition first published in 2003 by MBI Publishing
Company, Galtier Plaza, Suite 200
380 Jackson Street, St. Paul, MN 55101-3885 USA

The information in this book is true and complete to the best
of our knowledge. All recommendations are made without any
guarantee on the part of the author or publisher, who also
disclaim any liability incurred in connection with the use of
this data or specified details.

We recognize that some words, model names and designa-
tions, for example, mentioned herein are the property of the
trademark holder. We use them for identification purposes
only. This is not an official publication.

MBI Publishing Company books are also available at
discounts in bulk quantity for industrial or sales-promotional
use. For details write to Special Sales Manager at
Motorbooks International Wholesalers & Distributors,
Galtier Plaza, Suite 200, 380 Jackson Street, St. Paul,
MN 55101-3885 USA

ISBN 0-7603-1504-3

Editorial and design:
The Brown Reference Group plc
8 Chapel Place
Rivington Street
London
EC2A 3DQ
UK
www.brownreference.com

Printed in China

Senior Editor: Peter Darman
Editors: James Murphy, Alan Marshall
Picture Researchers: Susannah Jayes, Andrew Webb
Designer: Seth Grimbly
Production Director: Alastair Gourlay

PICTURE CREDITS
Aviation Photographs International: 49
Aviation Picture Library: 6, 9, 11, 12, 16, 17, 18, 32, 33,
37, 38, 39, 48, 49, 53, 57, 58, 60, 62, 64, 65, 67, 71,
79, 83, 84, 87, 89, 90, 91, 93, 94, 95
Defence Picture Library: 7, 20, 30
Chinese Defence Today (www.sinodefence.com): 13, 14, 15
Eurocopter: 22, 23, 24, 25, 26, 29, 31
Private Collection: 42, 56, 59, 63, 69, 72, 76
Howard Thacker: 68
The Flight Collection@Quadrant: 45, 52
Sikorsky: 88
TRH Pictures: 8, 10, 41, 47, 50, 54, 55, 61, 81, 82
US Coast Guard: 85
US Department of Defense: 35, 70, 73, 74, 75, 77, 78,
80, 86, 92
Simon Watson: 43, 44
Mark Wagner@aviationimages.com: 66
Westland Helicopters: 19, 27, 28, 34
Wingman Aviation: 40, 46

CONTENTS

SH-2G SUPER SEASPRITE

The SH-2G Super Seasprites of the Royal Australian Navy (RAN) operate from the ANZAC class frigate, mainly in the primary operational role of surface warfare. Accordingly, the aircraft is equipped with state-of-the-art Forward Looking Infra-Red (FLIR) electronic surveillance and protection equipment, a highly capable multi-mode radar, a cabin-mounted machine gun and the Kongsberg Penguin anti-ship missile. The SH-2G has a crew of two. However, it can also be flown by a single pilot and sensor operator (SENSO), due to the flexible Integrated Tactical Avionics System (ITAS) designed by Kaman and Litton Guidance & Controls. The SH-2G also supports underwater warfare operations by acting as a weapons carrier for other aircraft and ships equipped appropriately to locate and track submarines. The SH-2G is able to detect submarines on or near the surface using its FLIR, radar and Electronic Support Measures (ESM), but is not equipped with acoustic detection equipment. The helicopter can carry a variety of air-deliverable anti-submarine weapons, including lightweight torpedoes and depth charges. Like all RAN helicopters, the SH-2G is capable of many utility operations such as personnel and cargo transport, search and rescue (SAR), and external load-lifting. It can also be used to insert special operations forces covertly.

SPECIFICATIONS

Manufacturer:	Kaman Aerospace
Mission:	ASW, anti-ship
Length:	13.5m (44ft)
Height:	4.6m (15ft)
Rotor Diameter:	13.5m (44ft)
Crew:	2
Propulsion:	2 x GE T700-401
Horsepower:	3300 shaft horsepower
Maximum Speed:	256km/h (159mph)
Cruise Speed:	222km/h (138mph)
Vertical Rate of Climb:	630m/min (2070ft/min)
Range:	1000km (620 miles)
Weight:	3447kg (7600lb)
Date Deployed:	2001
Guns:	cabin-mounted machine gun
Missiles:	Penguin anti-ship missile, torpedo
Systems:	GPS, FLIR, ITAS, ESM

DEFENDER 500

AUS-made foreign military sales helicopter, the Defender 500 is a variant of the successful OH-6 series. It is used mainly by the armed forces, being very flexible and offering good all-round capabilities. Its missions differ from that of the OH-6 in that it takes on more roles, including direct air support, anti-tank, reconnaissance, observation and light utility. To this end, the Defender 500 can be equipped with a full complement of weapons systems, and configured either as a Defender Scout or as a Defender TOW (Tube launched, Optical tracked and Wire-guided) anti-tank platform. The Scout variation can be fitted with guns, 70mm Folding Fin Aerial Rockets (FFAR) and a grenade launcher. The TOW version can be fitted with twin TOW pods. To complement its increased firepower, the Defender 500 allows for the mounting of a stabilized, direct-view optical sight in the windshield. Options exist to fit a mast-mounted, multiple field-of-view optical sight, a target tracker, a laser rangefinder, thermal imager, a 16x FLIR for night navigation or targeting, and autopilot. This aircraft is used by 22 countries, ranging from the US through Iraq to El Salvador. It is an effective, flexible and relatively cheap helicopter, capable of delivering good results. However, it is no match for more advanced aircraft that have been developed to excel in specific roles.

SPECIFICATIONS

Manufacturer:	*The Boeing Company*
Mission:	*armed multi-purpose*
Length:	*7.6m (25ft)*
Height:	*2.6m (8ft)*
Rotor Diameter:	*8m (26ft)*
Crew:	*2*
Propulsion:	*1 x Allison T63-A-700*
Horsepower:	*317 shaft horsepower*
Maximum Speed:	*241km/h (149mph)*
Cruise Speed:	*221km/h (137mph)*
Vertical Rate of Climb:	*504m/min (1654ft/min)*
Range:	*485km (301 miles)*
Weight:	*896kg (1975lb)*
Date Deployed:	*1962*
Guns:	*40mm grenade launcher, mini-gun*
Missiles:	*TOW, 70mm FFAR*
Systems:	*GPS, FLIR, thermal imager*

CH-113 LABRADOR

Canada's twin-engined CH-113 Labrador helicopter has long been the workhorse of the country's SAR efforts. Originally brought into service in the early 1960s as the Voyageur, it was intended initially to support the Canadian Army. However, it was soon reconfigured from a tactical role to SAR duties, and its name was changed to Labrador. The helicopter has never been configured for military operations per se, but has seen action alongside the Royal Canadian Navy. It is designed with a watertight hull, making it suitable for marine landings. Standard equipment on this rescue craft includes a rescue hoist, a 3500l (770-gallon) long-range fuel tank and a cargo hook capable of holding a 5000kg (11,000lb) load. In addition to these features, the Labrador carries a full complement of emergency medical equipment. It has been at the forefront of SAR operations for the past 35 years, involved in some of the most demanding rescue attempts ever undertaken. The Labrador was used during Operation Saguenay in Quebec, when 14,000 people were evacuated from their flood-ravaged homes. However, the Canadian Government has decided to replace the ageing Labrador with the Cormorant (an adapted version of the EH-101 Merlin). The first one was delivered in 2002, with plans to have 15 in place by 2003.

SPECIFICATIONS

Manufacturer:	The Boeing Company
Mission:	SAR
Length:	25.4m (84ft)
Height:	5.0m (16ft)
Rotor Diameter:	2 x 15.2m (52ft)
Crew:	5
Propulsion:	2 x GE T-58-8F
Horsepower:	2800 shaft horsepower
Maximum Speed:	275km/h (171mph)
Vertical Rate of Climb:	not available
Cruise Speed:	235km/h (147mph)
Range:	1110km (687 miles)
Weight:	9707kg (21,355lb)
Date Deployed:	1967
Guns:	none
Missiles:	none
Systems:	GPS, rescue hoist

CH-124 SEA KING ASW

The CH-124 Sea King ASW (Anti-Submarine Warfare) is a ship-based helicopter with both day- and night-flight capabilities. It is carried aboard many Canadian Maritime Command destroyers, frigates and replenishment ships. The Sea King ASW carries detection, navigation and weapons systems to support its mandate of searching for, locating and destroying submarines. With its sub-surface acoustic detection equipment and homing torpedoes, it is also a versatile surveillance helicopter. In Canada, Sea Kings have become increasingly responsible for SAR operations and disaster relief. They also assist other government departments in carrying out anti-drugs operations, as well as fisheries and pollution patrols. The aircraft has also been instrumental in peacekeeping operations. For example, during the deployment of forces to Somalia, the CH-124 provided troops with logistics, medical and ammunition support, while also flying overland reconnaissance and convoy missions. It was, in effect, the only link soldiers had with the ships, especially during the initial stages of the deployment. This variation of the Sea King family is still used by the Canadian Royal Navy as its principal ASW helicopter, whereas other modern navies have begun to withdraw the Sea King from ASW roles, using them as utility transports.

SPECIFICATIONS

Manufacturer:	*Sikorsky Aircraft*
Mission:	*ASW*
Length:	*22.2m (72ft)*
Height:	*5.1m (16ft)*
Rotor Diameter:	*18.9m (62ft)*
Crew:	*4*
Propulsion:	*2 x GE T-58*
Horsepower:	*2800 shaft horsepower*
Maximum Speed:	*267km/h (166mph)*
Cruise Speed:	*167km/h (104mph)*
Vertical Rate of Climb:	*435m/min (1435ft/min)*
Range:	*616km (991 miles)*
Weight:	*5382kg (11,865lb)*
Date Deployed:	*1963*
Guns:	*1 x 7.62mm machine gun*
Missiles:	*Mk.46 homing torpedoes*
Systems:	*GPS, MAD*

CH-146 GRIFFON

Used exclusively by the Canadian armed forces, the CH-146 Griffon is a customized version of the popular Bell 412 helicopter. It is used as Canada's Utility Transport Tactical Helicopter (UTTH) and provides a robust, reliable and cost-effective capability. Its duties include airlift of equipment and personnel, command and liaison flights, surveillance and reconnaisance, casualty evacuation, logistic transport, SAR, anti-drugs tasks and domestic relief operations. The Griffon is the workhorse of the Canadian armed forces. It has been involved in conducting humanitarian relief operations at home and abroad, including Operation Saguenay in Quebec during the floods of 1996 and in Honduras in 1998. The aircraft is also used to support annual maintenance on the High Arctic Data Communications System (HADACS) on Ellesmere Island. The CH-146 has seen action in Haiti as part of the United Nations mission, as well as supporting NATO in Kosovo. This helicopter is used primarily for tactical lift and transportation purposes and, as a result, carries no weaponry other than two machine guns for self-defence. However, it can be configured for many different roles including logistic airlift, aero-medical support and casualty evacuation, reconnaissance and surveillance, fire-fighting and communications assistance.

SPECIFICATIONS

Manufacturer:	Bell Helicopter Textron
Mission:	utility tactical
Length:	17.1m (56ft)
Height:	4.6m (15ft)
Rotor Diameter:	14m (46ft)
Crew:	3
Propulsion:	2 x Pratt & Whitney PT6T-3D
Horsepower:	1800 shaft horsepower
Maximum Speed:	260km/h (160mph)
Cruise Speed:	220km/h (136mph)
Vertical Rate of Climb:	409m/min (1350 ft/min)
Range:	656km (408 miles)
Weight:	3363kg (7400lb)
Date Deployed:	1995
Guns:	2 x 7.62mm machine guns
Missiles:	none
Systems:	GPS, FLIR

CH-149 CORMORANT

A collaborative effort between Britain's Westland Helicopters and Agusta of Italy produced the CH-149 Cormorant. The offspring of these two well-established helicopter manufacturers is one of the most capable aircraft in the world today. Known elsewhere as the Merlin, the aircraft in Canadian service is called the Cormorant. This helicopter has been ordered and delivered to a number of armed forces within the European theatre, including the British Royal Navy. It has also been ordered by Canada as a SAR helicopter, replacing the elderly CH-113 Labrador. The Canadian version is based on the EH-101 Merlin, and saw off other US and European competitors in the Canadian SAR procurement drive. It is capable of operating in the most challenging of conditions, a vital prerequisite for any Canadian helicopter given the harsh climate. The Cormorant has a range and endurance far beyond its Canadian SAR predecessors. It has no military equipment onboard, thanks to its exclusive SAR role, yet it works closely with many other elements of the Canadian armed forces. The CH-149 is an extremely capable aircraft, representing an important addition to the Canadian SAR fleet and becoming a fitting replacement for the long-serving Labrador.

SPECIFICATIONS

Manufacturer:	E H Industries
Mission:	SAR
Length:	22.8m (75ft)
Height:	6.7m (22ft)
Rotor Diameter:	18.6m (61ft)
Crew:	3
Propulsion:	3 x GE T700-T6A1
Horsepower:	6700 shaft horsepower
Maximum Speed:	296km/h (185mph)
Cruise Speed:	275km/h (173mph)
Vertical Rate of Climb:	510m/min (1530ft/min)
Range:	926km (580 miles)
Weight:	7121kg (15,700lb)
Date Deployed:	2002
Guns:	none
Missiles:	none
Systems:	GPS, FLIR, winch

S-70

Unlike many Chinese People's Liberation Army (PLA) aircraft, which are generally inferior copies of Western models, the S-70 is a legitimate original helicopter sold to China by the US during the 1980s. The sale of 24 S-70C Black Hawks to the PLA in 1985 took place during a period of flourishing US/China military relations. This sophisticated aircraft is still used by the PLA, and represents one of China's most prized military assets. As the best helicopter in PLA service, the fast and manoeuvrable S-70C has received much care and attention, along with special enhancements that include the LTN3100VLF weather radar/navigation system and more powerful General Electric T700-701A engines. Remarkably, it is the only helicopter in PLA service that can fly in Tibet's harsh weather conditions. However, due to the deterioration in relations between the US and China, with sanctions in place since 1990, the Black Hawks have been starved of the parts needed to keep them in perfect flying order. It is thought that only a few remain in operating condition. China may be hoping shortly to receive spare parts from the US for these prized aircraft, but details of their condition and current military use are scarce. It is difficult, therefore, to predict the future of the PLA's S-70 Black Hawks.

SPECIFICATIONS

Manufacturer:	Sikorsky Aircraft
Mission:	utility
Length:	19.5m (64ft)
Height:	4.8m (16ft)
Rotor Diameter:	16.5m (53ft)
Crew:	2
Propulsion:	2 x GE T700-701A
Horsepower:	3400 shaft horsepower
Maximum Speed:	296km/h (184mph)
Cruise Speed:	257km/h (160mph)
Vertical Rate of Climb:	472m/min (1550ft/min)
Range:	584km (363 miles)
Weight:	5224 kg (11,516lb)
Date Deployed:	1985
Guns:	2 x 7.62mm machine guns
Missiles:	none
Systems:	LTN3100VLF weather radar

SA 342L GAZELLE

China's PLA obtained eight SA 342L Gazelle anti-tank attack helicopters in the late 1980s. It was part of the Chinese Army's preparation to resist a possible invasion by Soviet armoured troops from the northern border. As the PLA's first generation of attack helicopters, this tiny fleet was used to study and test various anti-tank tactics, giving the PLA invaluable experience of modern anti-armour warfare. The purchase of more units and licensed production were considered, but the end of the Cold War and the restoration of the Sino-Soviet relationship terminated the programme. The Eurocopter/Aerospatiale SA 341/342 Gazelle is a French-built light utility helicopter first flown in 1967. Military missions include attack, anti-tank, anti-helicopter, reconnaissance, utility, transport and training. Like the Chinese S-70, the SA 342L Gazelle has not been copied or reproduced, but still remains in service, often acting as enemy aircraft in exercises. As relations between France and China remain friendly, spare parts and the required maintenance are available. The Gazelle is an exceptionally swift and nimble aircraft which, though lacking the punching-power of heavier or more specialized helicopters, is highly capable. A number of first-rate military powers, including Britain and France, still have the Gazelle in active service.

SPECIFICATIONS

Manufacturer:	Eurocopter
Mission:	anti-tank, ground attack
Length:	11.9m (39ft)
Height:	3.1m (10ft)
Rotor Diameter:	10.5m (34ft)
Crew:	1/2
Propulsion:	1 x Turbomeca IIIB
Horsepower:	600 shaft horsepower
Maximum Speed:	310km/h (193mph)
Cruise Speed:	270km/h (168mph)
Vertical Rate of Climb:	732m/min (2415ft/min)
Range:	735km (459 miles)
Weight:	998kg (2195lb)
Date Deployed:	1987
Guns:	1 x 7.62mm machine gun
Missiles:	HOT, HJ-8 ATM
Systems:	basic flight systems

Z-8

The Z-8 is a Chinese copy of the Eurocopter SA 321 Super Frelon. The licensed manufacturer, Changhe Aircraft Industry Corporation, began the reverse engineering work of the Super Frelon in 1976. The first flight of the Chinese-made version, designated Z-8, took place on 11 December 1985. However, due to a variety of technical problems, only a small number of Z-8s (fewer than 20) have been built 18 years after the first flight. All are operated by the PLA's naval aviation arm. Due to the limitations of its large size, the Z-8 can be stationed only on large replenishment ships or on land airfields. A modified army variant called the Z-8A has been developed but has not yet entered service. Photographs of recent PLA joint exercises showed that some Z-8s were being used to transport and drop marine commandos in the enemy zone, illustrating that they are still an important part of the PLA. While the aircraft has largely been replaced by most first-rate military powers, the Chinese version of the Super Frelon may remain in service for some time. The helicopter can be fitted with a wide range of equipment. For ASW missions, the Z-8 can carry the French-made Thomson Sintra HS-12 dipping sonar. It can also tow a minesweeping countermeasure system for mine clearance, or carry eight 250kg (550lb) mines.

SPECIFICATIONS

Manufacturer:	Changhe Aircraft Industry Corp.
Mission:	ASW
Length:	23m (75ft)
Height:	6.7m (22ft)
Rotor Diameter:	18.9m (62ft)
Crew:	2/3
Propulsion:	3 x WZ-6
Horsepower:	4250 shaft horsepower
Maximum Speed:	315km/h (196mph)
Cruise Speed:	266km/h (166mph)
Vertical Rate of Climb:	300m/min (984ft/min)
Range:	830km (518 miles)
Weight:	3447kg (7600lb)
Date Deployed:	1985
Guns:	none
Missiles:	Yu-7 torpedo
Systems:	dipping sonar, minesweeping gear

Z-9W/G

China's Z-9W/G is the first indigenous anti-tank attack helicopter derived from the license-built Eurocopter AS 565N Panther. Its main armaments are four HJ-8 wire-guided anti-tank guided missiles (ATGMs) with a range of 600–3000m (1968–9842ft). The Z-9G is a modified formal production version derived from the Z-9W. In addition to the four HJ-8 ATGMs, the Z-9G can also carry two 57mm rocket launchers or two 12.7mm machine gun pods. The HJ-8 ATGM is guided by a roof-mounted optical sight for searching and tracking. At the Zhuhai Airshow in 2000, China revealed its TY-90 short-range air-to-air missile (AAM), which is designed specifically for helicopter air combat. This missile could eventually be fitted to the Z-9G. Unlike previous Chinese attempts to copy Western designs, the Z-9 is a genuine effort to license-build the country's own aircraft. To a large extent, China has succeeded with this helicopter. However, there is a question mark over the country's ability to provide the necessary spares and ongoing engineering expertise. Considerable effort has gone into the development of this anti-tank helicopter, but only time will tell if it is successful. It isn't certain that China faces any threat requiring anti-armour capability, but the PLA is still attempting to modernize its aviation armoury.

SPECIFICATIONS

Manufacturer:	*Harbin Aircraft Manufacturing*
Mission:	*anti-tank*
Length:	*13.5m (44ft)*
Height:	*3.5m (12ft)*
Rotor Diameter:	*14m (46ft)*
Crew:	*1/2*
Propulsion:	*2 x Turbomeca Arriel 1C2*
Horsepower:	*1400 shaft horsepower*
Maximum Speed:	*305km/h (190mph)*
Cruise Speed:	*255km/h (159mph)*
Vertical Rate of Climb:	*420m/min (1400ft/min)*
Range:	*1000km (625 miles)*
Weight:	*2050kg (4510lb)*
Date Deployed:	*1995*
Guns:	*2 x 12.7mm machine guns*
Missiles:	*HJ-8 ATGM, 57mm rockets, AAM*
Systems:	*roof-mounted optical sight*

Z-11

The Z-11 is a Chinese copy of the French AS-350B Ecureuil light helicopter, which was developed in the early 1970s. The programme was officially approved in 1989, and development began in 1992. The first flight of the Z-11 took place in December 1994. It is designed for training, scout, liaison and rescue missions, as well as various civil tasks. Although described by the manufacturer as multi-mission, the future of the helicopter is uncertain due to its limited take-off weight, insufficient armament, low survivability and outdated technology. So far the PLA has ordered only a few (no more than 20) Z-11s for pilot training. The quality of the Chinese copies of Western aircraft often lack genuine airworthiness, and China has generally failed in its attempts to produce an indigenous helicopter capable of meaningful military operations. However, the tactic of buying a few foreign helicopters to copy lives on, despite the obvious drawbacks. The Ecureuil helicopter, as manufactured by Eurocopter, is a popular aircraft the world over, in service with myriad defence agencies. This is testimony to the utility of the design, but the Chinese imitation perhaps lacks the finesse and quality of the original, thereby reducing the military value of the helicopter. The PLA's apparent lack of enthusiasm is leaving the aircraft on the sidelines.

SPECIFICATIONS

Manufacturer:	*Changhe Aircraft Industry Corp.*
Mission:	*light support*
Length:	*13m (43ft)*
Height:	*3.1m (10ft)*
Rotor Diameter:	*13m (43ft)*
Crew:	*2*
Propulsion:	*1 x WZ-8D*
Horsepower:	*not available*
Maximum Speed:	*278km/h (173mph)*
Cruise Speed:	*230km/h (143mph)*
Vertical Rate of Climb:	*474m/min (1555ft/min)*
Range:	*560km (350 miles)*
Weight:	*1120kg (2464lb)*
Date Deployed:	*1994*
Guns:	*none*
Missiles:	*none*
Systems:	*basic flight systems*

A109 HIRUNDO

High power provided by the A109 Military's twin engines makes it a robust and versatile aircraft. It is a lightweight, eight-seat, multi-purpose helicopter, manufactured by Italy's Agusta. The power available allows mission continuation even in the event of one engine failure. This, together with systems duplication and separation, gives the A109 the survivability necessary for military operations. The integrated 1553 military standard digital data bus-compatible mission equipment package, with the wide range of armament and day/night Target Acquisition & Designation Sight (TADS), makes the A109 a real multi-role light helicopter able to satisfy most military requirements. This versatility allows the aircraft to fill different roles such as anti-tank, scout, light attack, escort, area suppression, patrol and reconnaissance missions, plus transport of men and materials. The A109 is powered by two Pratt & Whitney PW-206C or two Turbomeca Arrius 2K1 turboshaft engines, both with a Full Authority Digital Eletronic Control (FADEC) system. These are mounted side by side and drive a combining gearbox. The A109 is currently in service with the Italian armed forces, as well as in Greece, Argentina, Venezuela and with the British special forces. It is well suited to competing in the cut-throat military procurement arena, given its inherent flexibility and all-round performance.

SPECIFICATIONS

Manufacturer:	*Agusta*
Mission:	*multi-role*
Length:	*13m (43ft)*
Height:	*3.3m (10ft)*
Rotor Diameter:	*11m (36ft)*
Crew:	*1/2*
Propulsion:	*2 x Turbomeca Arrius 2K1*
Horsepower:	*800 shaft horsepower*
Maximum Speed:	*305km/h (190mph)*
Cruise Speed:	*265km/h (165mph)*
Vertical Rate of Climb:	*not available*
Range:	*565km (353 miles)*
Weight:	*1415kg (3113lb)*
Date Deployed:	*1974*
Guns:	*2 x 7.62mm machine guns*
Missiles:	*HOT, TOW, FFAR rockets*
Systems:	*GPS, FLIR, FADEC*

A129 MANGUSTA

The Italian Army's A129 Mangusta (Mongoose), armed with anti-tank and area-suppression weapons systems, is intended primarily as an attack helicopter to be used against armoured targets. The aircraft can operate during day, night and all-weather conditions. The A129 Mangusta claims to be a proven hot-climate operator, as demonstrated during its peacekeeping operations – it was employed successfully in Somalia where it proved highly reliable and extremely flexible. When Agusta of Italy developed the Mongoose, it became the first attack helicopter to be designed and produced wholly in Europe. Italy is the only country with this helicopter in its inventory. An escort/scout version of the Mangusta is under development for deployment with airmobile units. The aircraft would also be armed for air-to-air combat. The A129 International, developed from the Mangusta, meets the requirements of today's armed forces for a multi-role combat helicopter that combines high performance and survivability with low support costs. Though it lacks the firepower and technological capabilities of peers such as the AH-1 Cobra or the AH-64D Apache Longbow, it is nonetheless a capable aircraft which can be bought at a much lower cost than its US counterparts.

SPECIFICATIONS

Manufacturer:	Agusta
Mission:	light attack
Length:	14.3m (47ft)
Height:	3.4m (11ft)
Rotor Diameter:	11.9m (39ft)
Crew:	2
Propulsion:	2 x Piaggio Gem 2 Mk1004D
Horsepower:	1500 shaft horsepower
Maximum Speed:	313km/h (196mph)
Cruise Speed:	240km/h (150mph)
Vertical Rate of Climb:	612m/min (979ft/min)
Range:	700km (437 miles)
Weight:	2520kg (5575lb)
Date Deployed:	2001
Guns:	2 x 20mm machine guns
Missiles:	HOT, TOW, Stinger, rockets
Systems:	GPS, FLIR

AH-7 LYNX

Westland's legendary Lynx is one of the most successful light anti-shipping/submarine helicopters ever built, and has been exported to many countries. The British Army, along with the armed forces of many other nations, has adapted the Lynx design to an anti-tank role, armed in this instance with TOW missiles. Due to its cutting-edge technology semi-rigid titanium rotor-head, the aircraft is superbly manoeuvrable and fast. A stripped-down Lynx still holds the world record for the highest speed achieved by a helicopter. The aircraft is adaptable to a wide variety of missions, contributing to its worldwide popularity. Originally, 113 Lynx AH Mk 1s were supplied to Britain's Army Air Corps as a multi-role helicopter. However, during the Cold War its primary job was as an anti-tank aircraft, given its ability to carry eight TOW anti-tank missiles plus a further eight in the cabin as a reload – a vast improvement over the AH-1 Scout it replaced. The latest Lynx in UK Army Air Corps service is the AH Mk 9, designed as a Light Battlefield Helicopter (LBH). It is an integral part of the hard-hitting new 16th Air Assault Brigade. Despite the Lynx's advanced age, it is likely to remain in service for several more years, although the newer Merlin and Apache helicopters can be expected to take over some of its roles.

SPECIFICATIONS

Manufacturer:	Westland Helicopters
Mission:	anti-tank
Length:	12m (39ft)
Height:	3.4m (11ft)
Rotor Diameter:	12.8m (42ft)
Crew:	2
Propulsion:	2 x Rolls-Royce Gem 41
Horsepower:	1800 shaft horsepower
Maximum Speed:	330km/h (206mph)
Cruise Speed:	232km/h (145mph)
Vertical Rate of Climb:	604m/min (1994ft/min)
Range:	528km (330 miles)
Weight:	3291kg (7240lb)
Date Deployed:	1962
Guns:	2 x 7.62mm machine guns
Missiles:	TOW
Systems:	GPS

AS 355N ECUREUIL

Eurocopter has found the manufacture of the Ecureuil to be something of a cash cow. It is in service with armed forces, police forces, rescue units and civilian flight schools the world over. More than 3000 of these very adaptable helicopters have been sold internationally. Five UK police forces have already adopted the AS 355N for their operations, but Britain does not operate the Ecureuil in a military role. The major attraction of the AS 355N is the high power provided by its twin Turbomeca Arrius 1A turboshafts, which develop maximum take-off power of 579 shaft horsepower. The low vibration level also helps to reduce noise, a major consideration in urban night-time flying. The spacious cabin of the Ecureuil allows mission-specific equipment to be integrated while retaining excellent visibility. Many of these aircraft in service with law enforcement agencies carry a thermal imaging camera, FLIR and a TV camera package mounted under the machine's nose. They may also have a Nightsun searchlight capable of illuminating a large area from a signficant altitude. The Ecureuil does see military service in France, where it is used as a light utility aircraft in reconnaissance missions, or for command-and-control purposes. Normally without weapons, it can be armed with a machine gun for self-defence if required.

SPECIFICATIONS

Manufacturer:	Eurocopter
Mission:	lightweight utility
Length:	10.9 m (36ft)
Height:	3.1 m (10ft)
Rotor Diameter:	10.7m (35ft)
Crew:	1/2
Propulsion:	2 x Turbomeca Arrius 1A
Horsepower:	579 shaft horsepower
Maximum Speed:	224km/h (140mph)
Cruise Speed:	200km/h (125mph)
Vertical Rate of Climb:	390m/min (1287ft/min)
Range:	700km (440 miles)
Weight:	1305kg (2871lb)
Date Deployed:	1985
Guns:	None
Missiles:	None
Systems:	GPS, FLIR, searchlight

AS 532 COUGAR

The AS 532 Cougar Mk II U2 A2 helicopter has the biggest cabin volume in its category, capable of transporting 29 commandos or 12 stretchers with medical equipment. In addition, it is capable of carrying 5000kg (11,000lb) under-slung on the hook. This version is tasked primarily with combat SAR missions, retrieving downed pilots or special forces teams from deep behind enemy lines, or evacuating injured troops in dangerous battle zones. There is also an armed version, which can be equipped with a 20mm cannon or two pintle-mounted .50in machine guns. Its basic design, with screens in the cockpit and a four-axis autopilot with built-in coupler, makes it possible to reduce the crew workload and increase its safety for tactical flight by the same degree. This highly effective aircraft is primarily in service with the French armed forces, but has also been ordered by Saudi Arabia. For very long-range missions, the combat SAR helicopter can carry auxiliary fuel tanks on the cargo hook. With additional tanks stored internally, the aircraft can travel up to 1120km (700 miles) and back, rescuing two people in the process. For extra endurance and even longer operational range, an in-flight refuelling capability is being developed by the manufacturer in order to boost the helicopter's already impressive performance.

SPECIFICATIONS

Manufacturer:	Eurocopter
Mission:	combat SAR
Length:	16.3m (54ft)
Height:	4.6m (15ft)
Rotor Diameter:	15.6m (51ft)
Crew:	2/3
Propulsion:	2 x Turbomeca Makila 1A2
Horsepower:	3800 shaft horsepower
Maximum Speed:	325km/h (203mph)
Cruise Speed:	262km/h (163mph)
Vertical Rate of Climb:	420m/min (1386ft/min)
Range:	842km (526 miles)
Weight:	4700kg (10,340lb)
Date Deployed:	1996
Guns:	20mm cannon
Missiles:	2.75in rockets
Systems:	GPS, FLIR

AS 532 COUGAR UL

Eurocopter's AS 532 Cougar UL is a multi-mission, twin-engined helicopter which is part of the Horizon radar surveillance system. This technology was developed to counter any possible threat posed by the tank fleets of the Warsaw Pact countries. The system includes a Cougar helicopter with radar and electronic countermeasures (ECM), plus a ground station. The first flight of the Horizon Cougar with the full radar system took place in late 1992, and the French Army took an initial delivery in July 1996. It is also in service with the Swiss Air Force, which ordered 27 aircraft. Another buyer of the Cougar UL is the Turkish Army. The helicopter is equipped with a long-range, multi-mode retractable pulse Doppler radar. A rotating antenna is carried beneath the fuselage, and the radar range is 200km (124 miles). The radar scans a ground area of 20,000km^2 (12,400 square miles) in 10 seconds, and the data is transmitted to a ground station. The information is then disseminated to relevant parties as a real-time snapshot of the situation on the ground. The Horizon-equipped Cougar reflects the new emphasis being placed on Command, Control, Communications and Intelligence (C3I) and the developing role of heliborne surveillance radar. The aircraft may be unarmed, but it is still an effective force multiplier.

SPECIFICATIONS

Manufacturer:	Eurocopter
Mission:	heliborne surveillance
Length:	16.3m (54ft)
Height:	4.6m (15ft)
Rotor Diameter:	15.6m (51ft)
Crew:	2/3
Propulsion:	2 x Turbomeca Makila 1A1
Horsepower:	3550 shaft horsepower
Maximum Speed:	325km/h (203mph)
Cruise Speed:	262km/h (163mph)
Vertical Rate of Climb:	420m/min (1386ft/min)
Range:	842km (526 miles)
Weight:	4700kg (10,340lb)
Date Deployed:	1996
Guns:	none
Missiles:	none
Systems:	GPS, Horizon radar system

AS 555 FENNEC

The AS 555 Fennec armed lightweight helicopter is a further development of the Aerospatiale AS 350, which flew for the first time in 1976. The Fennec is built by Eurocopter in France, and is used only by Denmark and Singapore. The AS 555 is normally configured for an anti-tank role but can be reconfigured into an unarmed version. It is equipped for instrument flying and can therefore operate in most weather conditions. The crew comprises a pilot and a gunner, who are both protected by armoured seats. In the anti-tank role, the Fennec is equipped with the weapons system HeliTOW. It consists of two TOW launchers with room for two TOW missiles each, an optical sight with 3x or 12x enlargement, a number of computers for calculations, and a control panel placed in front of the gunner. The maximum TOW range is 3.75km (2.4 miles). The Fennec is characterized by the ability to deploy fast and change targets quickly. It can also deploy in a night reconnaissance role as the crew are equipped with Pilots' Night Vision Goggles (PNVG). A major disadvantage of the Fennec is its ineffectiveness against stationary, camouflaged or dug-in targets because they cannot be recognized at long distances by the optical sight – and the helicopter lacks any other method of long-range detection.

SPECIFICATIONS

Manufacturer:	Eurocopter
Mission:	anti-tank
Length:	12.9m (42ft)
Height:	3.2m (11ft)
Rotor Diameter:	10.7m (35ft)
Crew:	1/2
Propulsion:	2 x Turbomeca Arrius 319-1
Horsepower:	520 shaft horsepower
Maximum Speed:	278km/h (173mph)
Cruise Speed:	217km/h (136mph)
Vertical Rate of Climb:	not available
Range:	666km (420 miles)
Weight:	1382kg (3040lb)
Date Deployed:	1993
Guns:	machine guns, 20mm cannon
Missiles:	TOW, rockets
Systems:	GPS, optical sight, PNVG

AS 565 PANTHER

The AS 565 Panther is the military version of the popular Dauphin helicopter as used by the US Coast Guard. It is capable of transporting up to 10 fully armed commandos into combat zones, performing casualty evacuation and providing logisitical support. The AS 565 SB is the armed version of the shipborne Panther. It can be carried on board a combat vessel such as a destroyer or frigate to improve the vessel's observation, reconnaissance and attack capabilities – augmenting the ship's original detection systems. This Eurocopter-built aircraft can carry a wide variety of weapons, including the MISTRAL and HOT missiles, as well as 70mm FFAR rockets. With a four-blade main rotor, two turboshaft engines are mounted side-by-side on top of the cabin. The teardrop-shaped body features a tapered boom to the tail fin, a rounded nose and stepped-up cockpit. The Panther has a retractable undercarriage and flat underside. The helicopter's tail flats have swept-back tips, mounted forward of the tapered fin. The rotor is inside a housing at the bottom of the fin. A weapons-carrying platform is installed on some models. The Panther is deployed aboard the French Navy Cassard Class anti-air frigates. It is also in service with other countries, carrying out regular operations for the Israeli Defence Force among others.

SPECIFICATIONS

Manufacturer:	Eurocopter
Mission:	light multi-pupose
Length:	11.6m (38ft)
Height:	3.9m (13ft)
Rotor Diameter:	11.9m (39ft)
Crew:	2/3
Propulsion:	2 x Turbomeca Arriel IMI
Horsepower:	1600 shaft horsepower
Maximum Speed:	296km/h (184mph)
Cruise Speed:	275km/h (171mph)
Vertical Rate of Climb:	420m/min (1400ft/min)
Range:	875km (547 miles)
Weight:	2255kg (4970lb)
Date Deployed:	1989
Guns:	20mm cannon
Missiles:	MISTRAL, HOT, 70mm FFAR
Systems:	GPS, FLIR. ORB-32 radar

EC 635

Eurocopter's EC 635 Light Utility Helicopter (LUH) is the military version of its EC 135 and features the same technology. The EC 635 is a modern, lightweight, twin-engined, eight-seat, multi-role helicopter that makes extensive use of composite materials and crash-resistant seats and fuel system. New-generation, high-set main rotor and shrouded tail rotor systems (Fenestron-type) provide low noise and safe operation. High operational efficiency, adverse weather day/night operations, high performance with power reserve and an advanced maintenance concept are among the key features of the EC 635. Utilizing the aircraft's multi-role capability, the EC 635 is suitable for military and paramilitary operations including utility, training, troop transport, reconnaissance and SAR. Helicopters such as the EC 635, with their exceptional efficiency and great flexibility, have become firm favourites with governments seeking to minimize military expenditure while maintaining effective armed forces. Helicopters in this class promise more capability for less money. Though seldom able to compete with specialized aircraft that have been tailor-made for particular missions, the EC 635 can operate in varied roles with great efficiency. Deployed in 1999, it is due to enter widespread active service over the next few years.

SPECIFICATIONS

Manufacturer:	Eurocopter
Mission:	light utility
Length:	10.2m (33ft)
Height:	3.5m (11ft)
Rotor Diameter:	10.2m (33ft)
Crew:	1/2
Propulsion:	2 x Turbomeca Arrius 2B1
Horsepower:	711 shaft horsepower
Maximum Speed:	259km/h (161mph)
Cruise Speed:	235km/h (146mph)
Vertical Rate of Climb:	456m/min (1500ft/min)
Range:	675km (422 miles)
Weight:	1490kg (3284lb)
Date Deployed:	1999
Guns:	20mm cannon
Missiles:	70mm FFAR
Systems:	GPS

EC 725 COUGAR

The EC 725 medium-sized, twin-engine helicopter is the latest member of the Cougar family developed by Eurocopter. The French Air Force has a requirement for 14 EC 725s for the combat SAR role, and is scheduled to introduce three into service during 2003. This brand-new aircraft is suitable for a wide range of missions, ranging from tactical troop transport, special operations, SAR, combat SAR and maritime surveillance to humanitarian support, logistic ground support, medical evacuation and shipborne operations. The ferry flight range of the EC 725 Cougar is more than 1500km (925 miles). In the tactical troop transport role, the aircraft can carry 19 soldiers. In the combat SAR role, the EC 725 is able to rescue a downed aircrew at a radius of action of 400km (250 miles). The maximum seat capacity is two crew and 29 troops. The Advanced Helicopter Cockpit and Avionics System (AHCAS) includes an automatic flight control system developed by SAGEM, integrating the flight, navigation and tactical mission data. The helicopter is equipped with radar and FLIR for day- and night-time SAR capability. The navigation suite includes Doppler radar, GPS and inertial navigation system. The helicopter has an extensive weapons-carrying capability, and can be armed with a variety of machine guns and rockets.

SPECIFICATIONS

Manufacturer:	*Eurocopter*
Mission:	*multi-mission*
Length:	*16.3m (54ft)*
Height:	*4.6m (15ft)*
Rotor Diameter:	*16.2m (53ft)*
Crew:	*2*
Propulsion:	*2 x Turbomeca Makila*
Horsepower:	*3800 shaft horsepower*
Maximum Speed:	*325km/h (203mph)*
Cruise Speed:	*262km/h (163mph)*
Vertical Rate of Climb:	*420m/min (1386ft/min)*
Range:	*1480km (920 miles)*
Weight:	*4700kg (10,340lb)*
Date Deployed:	*2003*
Guns:	*2 x 7.65mm machine guns*
Missiles:	*2.75in rockets*
Systems:	*GPS, FLIR, PNVG, AHCAS*

EH 101 MERLIN

Agusta of Italy and Britain's Westland Helicopters, through a venture named EH Industries, collaborated in the design of the highly effective EH 101 Merlin. The joint effort resulted in one of the world's most capable rotary-wing aircraft. Its primary roles consist of ASW, utility transport and SAR. This variation of the Merlin will be replacing the ageing Sea King ASW used by Britain's Royal Navy for its on-board anti-submarine operations. To achieve its mission goals, the Merlin is equipped with some of the most sophisticated systems known to aviation. These include the Blue Kestrel 360-degree radar, allowing the Merlin to operate completely independently in the search for and destruction of targets. It requires no support from other aerial or surface platforms to deliver good results. The Merlin is exceptionally versatile, able to adapt its configuration rapidly to the changing environment and mission goals. Not only is the aircaft versatile in its operational capability, but it is also flexible in the areas it can cover. It is an all-weather, 24-hour-capable helicopter, able to withstand extremes of temperature of plus or minus 50°. The Merlin is recognized as an exceptional machine, and is expected to see service with many nations, and earn Westland much money from foreign export sales.

SPECIFICATIONS

Manufacturer:	EH Industries
Mission:	ASW
Length:	22.8m (75ft)
Height:	6.7m (22ft)
Rotor Diameter:	18.6m (61ft)
Crew:	3
Propulsion:	3 x Rolls-Royce/Turbomeca RTM
Horsepower:	6700 shaft horsepower
Maximum Speed:	296km/h (185mph)
Cruise Speed:	275km/h (173mph)
Vertical Rate of Climb:	510m/min (1530ft/min)
Range:	926km (580 miles)
Weight:	7121kg (15,700lb)
Date Deployed:	1998
Guns:	2 x 7.62mm machine guns
Missiles:	Sea Skua, lightweight torpedoes
Systems:	GPS, FLIR, Blue Kestrel 360° radar

HC-4 SEA KING

B ritain's Royal Marines make good use of the HC-4 Sea King Commando. Introduced in the late 1970s, it has seen service wherever the Royal Marines have been in action. It is based on the basic Sea King design, but has additional capabilities and features that differ from the ASW and Airborne Early Warning (AEW) Sea Kings. These include the ability to transport up to 2730kg (6000lb) of equipment slung under the aircraft (including the 105mm Light Gun), to carry 27 fully equipped troops, and to fly in all types of weather. The all-weather capability is an especially useful characteristic since Royal Marines frequently operate in the most hostile environments. In addition, the Sea King Commando can be armed with a 7.62mm General Purpose Machine Gun (GPMG). By some helicopter standards, the Commando has not been in service for a particularly long time. However, the Sea King design is ageing fast, and this highly successful aircraft is to be replaced by the more advanced EH-101 Merlin helicopter. This process has already begun, and will eventually equip the Royal Marines with an even more formidable aircraft. The Sea King Commando saw action during the 1991 Gulf War, where it served with distinction in a most demanding environment.

SPECIFICATIONS

Manufacturer:	*Westland Helicopters*
Mission:	*utility transport*
Length:	*22.1m (73ft)*
Height:	*5.1m (17ft)*
Rotor Diameter:	*18.9m (61ft)*
Crew:	*3*
Propulsion:	*2 x Rolls-Royce Gnome H-1400*
Horsepower:	*3000 shaft horsepower*
Maximum Speed:	*256km/h (160mph)*
Cruise Speed:	*208km/h (130mph)*
Vertical Rate of Climb:	*670m/min (2200ft/min)*
Range:	*1230km (764 miles)*
Weight:	*6202kg (13,672lb)*
Date Deployed:	*1979*
Guns:	*1 x 7.62mm machine gun*
Missiles:	*none*
Systems:	*GPS, basic flight systems*

NH-90

The NH-90 began life in the early 1980s under a European multinational development programme for a new multi-purpose transport and naval helicopter, intended to replace the elderly UH-1 Huey, Puma and Sea King aircraft. The NH-90 is designed for survivability, reliability and ease of maintenance. It can be fitted with a FLIR turret in the nose, as well as with defensive countermeasure aids. The NH-90 is available in two forms, the NATO Frigate Helicopter (NFH) and the Tactical Transport Helicopter (TTH). The NFH is intended for ASW and maritime surface warfare, though it can be used for SAR and transport roles. It has an automatic rotor and tail-folding system, plus a combat avionics suite, including a 360-degree search radar in a drum under the fuselage, magnetic anomaly detector (MAD) and dipping sonar or sonobuoys. The TTH variant lacks the offensive avionics systems of the NFH, though it is fitted with weather radar. It has infrared exhaust suppressors; armoured crew seats; a cable cutter; a PNVG-compatible cockpit; plus an optional rear-loading ramp. Standard crew is pilot and copilot, with a payload capacity of 20 troops, 12 stretchers and a light tactical vehicle or 2500kg (5500lb) of cargo. The TTH can be equipped with defensive armament such as chaff and flares, or even with an infrared jammer.

SPECIFICATIONS

Manufacturer:	*Eurocopter*
Mission:	*multi-role transport*
Length:	*16.1m (53ft)*
Height:	*5.4m (18ft)*
Rotor Diameter:	*16.3m (53ft)*
Crew:	*2*
Propulsion:	*2 x Rolls-Royce/Turbomeca*
Horsepower:	*3084 shaft horsepower*
Maximum Speed:	*300km/h (186mph)*
Cruise Speed:	*259km/h (160mph)*
Vertical Rate of Climb:	*480m/min (1584ft/min)*
Range:	*1204km (650 miles)*
Weight:	*6428kg (14,741lb)*
Date Deployed:	*2003*
Guns:	*none*
Missiles:	*MU-90 torpedo, Exocet missile*
Systems:	*sonobuoy, FLIR, MAD*

PAH-1

Also known as the BO 105, the PAH-1 is a lightweight, twin-engine, multi-role military helicopter built by Eurocopter. The military version includes the anti-tank variant, with weapon-carrying outriggers; as well as the scout version, which has a mast-mounted sight above the main rotor. Missions include direct air support, anti-tank, reconnaissance, SAR and transportation. In addition to reconnaissance, observation and surveillance missions, this helicopter is particularly suitable for carrying taskforces and casualties, thanks to its unpartitioned cabin/cargo area. The aircraft can be reconfigured with ease for different armed duties. The machine can support the following specific weapon systems: anti-tank missiles; rocket launchers; pod-mounted gun; gun turret; and side-firing machine gun. It has been in service since the early 1970s, and has seen action with more than 40 national armed forces in countries as diverse as Bahrain, Canada and Mexico. The Maritime Search & Surveillance (MSS) BO 105 CBS 5 is the shipborne version. This helicopter features a 360-degree surveillance and meteorological radar. It can also support an associated data recorder and transmitter system, a Doppler/GPS navigation control system, and is PNVG compatible. It can also carry lightweight torpedoes.

SPECIFICATIONS

Manufacturer:	Eurocopter
Mission:	anti-tank, utility
Length:	8.8m (29ft)
Height:	3.0m (10ft)
Rotor Diameter:	9.8m (32 ft)
Crew:	2
Propulsion:	2 x Allison 250-C20B
Horsepower:	3300 shaft horsepower
Maximum Speed:	242km/h (151mph)
Cruise Speed:	205km/h (128mph)
Vertical Rate of Climb:	450m/min (1485ft/min)
Range:	555km (345 miles)
Weight:	1913kg (4208lb)
Date Deployed:	1973
Guns:	1 x RH 202 20mm cannon
Missiles:	anti-tank missiles, rocket pods
Systems:	GPS, weather radar, autopilot

PAH-2 TIGER

The PAH-2 Tiger owes its existence to a German and French agreement to collaborate on the development of a new advanced-attack helicopter for their armed forces. Ultimately, they settled on two basic versions: an anti-tank model for both countries; and an escort/fire support model for France. The design of the Tiger is typical of contemporary attack helicopters. The slim fuselage seats two crew in a tandem, stepped cockpit. While the German model follows the general trend of placing the gunner in the front seat and the pilot aft, the French prefer the opposite seating arrangement. The Tiger makes extensive use of composite materials both for weight reduction and to improve survivability. Armament is carried on two stub wings, and the French escort model is equipped with a cannon turret under the nose. The French HAC and German UHT models are primarily anti-tank versions equipped with a mast-mounted site and armed with HOT-2 or Trigat missiles. The French HAP, on the other hand, is optimized for air defence and fire support. It is generally armed with a nose cannon turret and air-to-air missiles. The first Tigers were delivered in 2001, and will shortly become fully operational. The helicopter became more recognizable after it had a taste of stardom, featuring in the James Bond movie *Goldeneye*.

SPECIFICATIONS

Manufacturer:	*Eurocopter*
Mission:	*attack*
Length:	*14m (46ft)*
Height:	*4.3m (14ft)*
Rotor Diameter:	*13m (43ft)*
Crew:	*2*
Propulsion:	*2 x Turbomeca/Rolls-Royce MTR*
Horsepower:	*2570 shaft horsepower*
Maximum Speed:	*320km/h (200mph)*
Cruise Speed:	*230km/h (145mph)*
Vertical Rate of Climb:	*640m/min (2105ft/min)*
Range:	*725km (453 miles)*
Weight:	*3300kg (7275lb)*
Date Deployed:	*2001*
Guns:	*1 x GIAT 30mm cannon*
Missiles:	*Stinger, Mistral, Trigat, HOT, FFAR*
Systems:	*GPS, FLIR*

SA 319 ALOUETTE III

No longer in service with most leading military powers, the Eurocopter-built SA 319 Alouette III multi-purpose and light-attack helicopter is a larger and very successful development of the earlier SE 313B Alouette II. In contrast to its predecessor, it has an improved structure, a stronger propulsion system, better equipment and a closed fuselage with cantilevers. The cabin is more spacious and can transport a larger payload. The military version is employed partly for its highly sensitive weapon and radar mechanisms. In an anti-shipping role, the SA 319B is equipped with ORB-31 radar and four AS.11/AS.12 missiles. For the purpose of ASW, the equipment available is the same radar, but with Crouzet MAD and two Mk 46 torpedos. The Alouette III has been phased out by the majority of first-rate military powers, and has been replaced by more modern helicopters. However, in its day the Alouette III was a cutting-edge aircraft. More than 1500 examples were sold in a production run lasting 20 years. A few of these aircraft are still used by less advanced or wealthy armed forces, and they continue to perform well. Romania and Switzerland, as well as India (which calls its licence-built version "Chetak"), still operate the Alouette III, though not generally in the light-attack role for which it was originally designed.

SPECIFICATIONS

Manufacturer:	*Eurocopter*
Mission:	*multi-purpose, light-attack*
Length:	*12.8m (42ft)*
Height:	*3m (10ft)*
Rotor Diameter:	*11m (33ft)*
Crew:	*1*
Propulsion:	*1 x Turbomeca Astazou XIV*
Horsepower:	*700 shaft horsepower*
Maximum Speed:	*220km/h (137mph)*
Cruise Speed:	*190km/h (118mph)*
Vertical Rate of Climb:	*258m/min (851ft/min)*
Range:	*600km (375 miles)*
Weight:	*1108kg (2437lb)*
Date Deployed:	*1973*
Guns:	*1 x 7.62mm machine gun*
Missiles:	*none*
Systems:	*basic flight systems*

SA 321 SUPER FRELON

The Super Frelon first flew in 1962 and began active service in 1966. This record-breaking helicopter was produced as a civilian transport version and in military transport, ASW and anti-ship guise. The Super Frelon is powered by three Turbomeca Turmo IIIC turbo-shafts married to a Fiat-built transmission system and Sikorsky-designed rotor head and blades. The six-blade main rotor is mounted above-centre of the fuselage. Of the three engines, two are mounted side-by-side atop the fuselage forward of the main rotor; the third is behind the main rotor. It has a boat hull-type fuselage that mounts stabilizing floats on either side of the body, which has fixed landing gear and an upswept rear section. The Super Frelon owes its existence to a French Ministry of Defence requirement for a large military troop transport helicopter, and was produced in both troop transport and ASW configurations. The successful aircraft was sold to a number of countries including Israel, South Africa and Libya. This powerful helicopter has broken several records, including the world speed record in 1963 at 341km/h (211mph) over 3km (2 miles) – unfortunately, now surpassed. The French Navy is beginning to phase out the Super Frelon, replacing it with the much more modern and capable Eurocopter-built NH-90 by 2005.

SPECIFICATIONS

Manufacturer:	*Eurocopter*
Mission:	*assault transport*
Length:	*23m (75ft)*
Height:	*6.7m (22ft)*
Rotor Diameter:	*18.9m (62ft)*
Crew:	*5*
Propulsion:	*3 x Turbomeca Turmo IIIC*
Horsepower:	*3150 shaft horsepower*
Maximum Speed:	*270km/h (168mph)*
Cruise Speed:	*248km/h (155mph)*
Vertical Rate of Climb:	*300m/min (984ft/min)*
Range:	*700km (437 miles)*
Weight:	*6863kg (15,098lb)*
Date Deployed:	*1966*
Guns:	*2 x 7.62mm machine guns*
Missiles:	*none*
Systems:	*GPS, IFF, PNVG*

SA 330 PUMA

Britain's Royal Air Force (RAF) first deployed the SA 330 Puma in 1971. This familiar helicopter was designed as a tactical transport vehicle; and various other versions, including the Super Puma, are now in service worldwide. Selection of the design arose from an RAF requirement to replace obsolete Belvedere and Whirlwind helicopters then in service. The Puma can operate as a casualty evacuation aircraft, transport for up to 16 fully equipped troops, and as a medium-lift transport carrying up to 2500kg (5500lb) of freight using under-fuselage hardpoints to sling loads externally. The Puma can also function effectively as a helicopter gunship capable of carrying a wide variety of armament. The aircraft is capable of being airlifted in a number of transport aircraft types with the minimum of work. Like the Chinook, the Puma is equipped with night vision aids, defensive ECM systems and advanced navigation aids. It is operated by many countries in various guises and configurations, although Britain and France are looking for a replacement for their ageing Puma fleets. The Puma has seen extensive operational use, including in the 1991 Gulf War, in the Balkans conflict and in counter-terrorist operations in Northern Ireland. It has been an asset to Britain's helicopter forces for three decades.

SPECIFICATIONS

Manufacturer:	*Westland Helicopters*
Mission:	*utility*
Length:	*15.5m (51ft)*
Height:	*4.92m (16ft)*
Rotor Diameter:	*15m (50ft)*
Crew:	*2*
Propulsion:	*2 x Turbomeca Makila*
Horsepower:	*3500 shaft horsepower*
Maximum Speed:	*278km/h (173mph)*
Cruise Speed:	*249km/h (155mph)*
Vertical Rate of Climb:	*420m/min (1386ft/min)*
Range:	*850km (531 miles)*
Weight:	*4370kg (9614lb)*
Date Deployed:	*1971*
Guns:	*1 x 7.62mm machine gun*
Missiles:	*none*
Systems:	*GPS, PNVG*

SA 341 GAZELLE

The Gazelle is another example of European collaboration in helicopter design and development. Designed primarily by Aerospatiale, the predecessor to the Eurocopter group, the British version was built under licence by Westland. The Gazelle is used by the British Army Air Corps, primarily as a scout helicopter, and designated the AH Mk1. It is small, light, exceptionally nimble and quick and is thus ideally suited to this role. It began life as an anti-tank helicopter, armed with missiles and rockets, although it has largely been replaced by more capable aircraft. The Gazelle was therefore re-designated as an observation and reconnaissance helicopter. It has seen action in almost every military confrontation in which British forces have been involved in since it came into service. It played a valuable amphibious role in the Falklands conflict, performed well in the deserts of Kuwait and Iraq, as well as operating effectively during the more recent Kosovo campaign. Indeed, it continues to serve in the reconnaissance role with the British Army, and can be expected to do so for some time. In the French Army, it is employed in a very similar scouting role to that in the UK. France, too, has found more modern and capable anti-tank helicopters, but still sees tangible battlefield value in the size, speed and agility of the Gazelle.

SPECIFICATIONS

Manufacturer:	Westland Helicopters
Mission:	reconnaissance
Length:	11.9m (39ft)
Height:	3.1m (10ft)
Rotor Diameter:	10.5m (34ft)
Crew:	1/2
Propulsion:	1 x Turbomeca Astazou XIVM
Horsepower:	600 shaft horsepower
Maximum Speed:	310km/h (193mph)
Cruise Speed:	270km/h (168mph)
Vertical Rate of Climb:	732m/min (2415ft/min)
Range:	670km (418 miles)
Weight:	998kg (2195lb)
Date Deployed:	1973
Guns:	1 x 7.62mm machine gun
Missiles:	HOT, 2.75in rockets
Systems:	PNVG, laser sight

WAH-64D APACHE

More than 60 WAH-64D Apache Longbow helicopters are being procured for the British Army. The aircraft is based on the Boeing AH-64D Apache Longbow which entered service with the US Army in 1998. The formidable surveillance and target acquisition capability of the sensor suite, together with other improvements in weapon systems and avionics, means that the Westland Apache will represent a significant increase in capability when compared with the Lynx Mk.7 TOW currently in service with the British Army. It will be a fully digitized platform which, when linked to other weapon systems, will be capable of revolutionizing the battlefield of the future. The Westland Apache presents a completely new capability, with implications for the British Army's organization, training, logistics and peace-time infrastructure. The Westland-built British Army version of the Apache has some special characteristics. The RTM322 engines offer significant improvement in performance, while the radio has been upgraded to the new digital BOWMAN system due to enter the British armed forces. Another UK-specific feature is HIDAS (Helicopter Integrated Defensive Aids System), developed by Marconi and providing an integrated suite of radar, laser and missile-warning sensors and countermeasures.

SPECIFICATIONS

Manufacturer:	Westland Helicopters
Mission:	attack
Length:	15.5m (51ft)
Height:	5m (16ft)
Rotor Diameter:	14.6m (48ft)
Crew:	2
Propulsion:	2 x RTM322
Horsepower:	3000 shaft horsepower
Maximum Speed:	360km/h (225mph)
Cruise Speed:	261km/h (163mph)
Vertical Rate of Climb:	737m/min (2432ft/min)
Range:	410km (256 miles)
Weight:	5352kg (11,774lb)
Date Deployed:	2001
Guns:	1 x M230 30mm chain gun
Missiles:	Hellfire, CRV-7, Stinger, Sidewinder
Systems:	FLIR, TADS, HIDAS, Longbow radar

WASP HAS 1

The Wasp was based on the British Army Scout helicopter and was originally named Sea Scout. Many trials were carried out with prototype aircraft to assess the viability of operating small helicopters in an anti-submarine role from frigates. When these trials were shown to be a success, greatly increasing such a ship's ASW capability, Britain's Royal Navy ordered the Wasp HAS 1. The first production model was delivered in 1963, and a total of 98 Wasp HAS 1s were ultimately built for the Royal Navy. The type served on Royal Navy frigates until the late 1970s when it was replaced by the Lynx. However, the Wasp had an unexpected reprieve in 1982 when several old frigates, incapable of operating the Lynx, were re-commissioned due to the Falklands conflict. Indeed, a Wasp helicopter aboard the Royal Navy frigate HMS *Plymouth* crippled the Argentine submarine *Santa Fe* in South Georgia at the start of the war, by firing an AS-12 missile through the submarine's conning tower. After this campaign, the Wasp was withdrawn from service when the last of the older frigates was decommissioned in 1988. While the Wasp is generally being replaced by more modern and capable aircraft, it still serves in many air forces and navies around the world, including those of Malaysia and New Zealand, although in ever-decreasing numbers.

SPECIFICATIONS

Manufacturer:	*Westland Helicopters*
Mission:	*light reconnaissance*
Length:	*12.9m (40ft)*
Height:	*2.7m (9ft)*
Rotor Diameter:	*9.8m (32ft)*
Crew:	*1/2*
Propulsion:	*1 x Rolls-Royce Bristol Nimbus 503*
Horsepower:	*710 shaft horsepower*
Maximum Speed:	*193km/h (120mph)*
Cruise Speed:	*179km/h (111mph)*
Vertical Rate of Climb:	*not available*
Range:	*670km (418 miles)*
Weight:	*1566kg (3452lb)*
Date Deployed:	*1963*
Guns:	*1 x 7.62mm machine gun*
Missiles:	*rockets, torpedoes*
Systems:	*basic flight systems*

WESSEX

The Wessex is the old lady of the British armed forces' helicopter fleet. It first flew in 1966 and continues in service to this day, though in a much reduced capacity. Originally used as a light support helicopter, Westland's Wessex was initially capable of carrying 12 fully equipped troops or 3500kg (7700lb) of underslung cargo, including light artillery pieces and vehicles. Based on the successful Sikorsky S-58 design, the Wessex has two different engines to increase its capabilities. The venerable aircraft has served with Britain's RAF for more than 30 years. Those aircraft still active are the last of around 60 ordered for the RAF, and are used as light support helicopters (and SAR units in Cyprus) capable of carrying an increased load of 16 fully equipped troops. Previous RAF roles included SAR, training and transport duties with The Queen's Flight. The Wessex also saw extensive action in the Falklands conflict, where it took part in a number of special forces actions with the Special Air Service (SAS) and Special Boat Service (SBS). In its SAR role, much of its time was spent in search of civilians who had become stranded at sea or lost on mountains. Although it was on 24-hour standby to rescue downed pilots, it excelled in rescuing civilians and undoubtedly saved hundreds of lives over the course of its operational life.

SPECIFICATIONS

Manufacturer:	Westland Helicopters
Mission:	SAR and support
Length:	14.7m (48ft)
Height:	4.9m (16ft)
Rotor Diameter:	17m (66ft)
Crew:	2
Propulsion:	2 x Rolls-Royce Gnome 112/113
Horsepower:	1600 shaft horsepower
Maximum Speed:	212km/h (132mph)
Cruise Speed:	195km/h (121mph)
Vertical Rate of Climb:	480m/min (1584ft/min)
Range:	630km (390 miles)
Weight:	3455kg (7600lb)
Date Deployed:	1966
Guns:	none
Missiles:	none
Systems:	not available

HAL DHRUV

Designed and developed by Hindustan Aeronautics Ltd (HAL), the Dhruv Advanced Light Helicopter (ALH) is a modern, efficient and highly cost-effective multi-role helicopter. It is an indigenously designed and developed aircraft, something of a rarity outside the US and Europe. The Dhruv was conceived to meet the requirements of the Indian Army, Navy, Air Force and the Coastguard. It has been designed with great flexibility in mind and, as such, it can be configured as an armed gunship, a utility transport, an ASW/anti-ship helicopter and a platform for SAR and casualty evacuation. The Dhruv, deployed in 2002, is powered by two Turbomeca TM-333 turbo-shaft engines procured from France. These units are being produced under licence in India by HAL. Large rear clamshell doors allow easy loading of stretchers or other bulky loads. It is simple to fly and economical to maintain. From its inception, the Dhruv has been designed in close cooperation with the military, bringing their expertise and requirements into the design process. With sonar/sonics, radar, ESM, torpedoes, depth charges and anti-ship missiles, the Dhruv can be an effective ASW or anti-shipping aircraft. Similarly, with the turret gun, rockets, air-to-air missiles and third-generation anti-tank missiles, it is also a useful battlefield asset.

SPECIFICATIONS

Manufacturer:	Hindustan Aeronautics Ltd
Mission:	light multi-role
Length:	12.9m (43ft)
Height:	3.4m (11ft)
Rotor Diameter:	13.2m (44ft)
Crew:	2
Propulsion:	2 x Turbomeca TM-333-2B
Horsepower:	1800 shaft horsepower
Maximum Speed:	280km/h (175mph)
Cruise Speed:	245km/h (153mph)
Vertical Rate of Climb:	540m/min (1782ft/min)
Range:	800km (500 miles)
Weight:	2505kg (5511lb)
Date Deployed:	2002
Guns:	2 x 20mm machine guns
Missiles:	ATGM, AAM, rockets, torpedoes
Systems:	GPS

MI-6 HOOK

When it was unveiled to the world in 1957, the Mil Mi-6 had no rival as the world's biggest helicopter. Designed as a large transport for military and commercial applications, the Mil Mi-6 stunned Western observers with its sheer size. NATO gave the giant helicopter the codename Hook. However, the Mi-6 is capable of carrying loads in other ways than merely using a hook. A two-winged rear door swings open to accommodate bulky loads. Additional cargoes can be attached externally. Extra fuel tanks are another option for attachment to two stubby wings extending sideways just aft of the rotor shaft, offering additional fuel capacity. The Mi-6 was produced mainly by the Kazan aircraft factory from 1968 until about 1980. As well as the Indian armed forces, buyers have been found in Belarus, Bulgaria, Egypt, Iraq, Poland, Peru and Vietnam. As spare parts for the huge transport aircraft have become expensive, the Mi-6 has been pushed out of the heavy-duty airlifting market by the newer and still larger Russian-built Mil Mi-26 Halo. A few Hooks can still be seen in Siberia, although many seem no longer to be airworthy. However, the Indian Air Force has kept a few of these ageing aircraft in service, though they have been largely replaced by the more modern Halo, which appears to be cheaper to maintain.

SPECIFICATIONS

Manufacturer:	Mil/Kazan
Mission:	heavy transport
Length:	33m (109ft)
Height:	9.7m (32ft)
Rotor Diameter:	35m (115ft)
Crew:	5
Propulsion:	2 x Soloviev D-25V
Horsepower:	10,850 shaft horsepower
Maximum Speed:	300km/h (186mph)
Cruise Speed:	250km/h (156 miles)
Vertical Rate of Climb:	not available
Range:	1000km (625 miles)
Weight:	27,240kg (60,054lb)
Date Deployed:	1959
Guns:	none
Missiles:	none
Systems:	internal auto-loading system

MI-25 HIND D

An export version of the standard Russian Mi-24 Hind D helicopter, India's Mi-25 Hind D isn't as modern as the Mi-35 export version of the Mi-24 Hind E. That said, there are very few differences between these individual aircraft, save varying avionics and doctrine. As with a great many nations around the world, the Indian armed forces have been attracted by the awesome firepower of the Hind series of helicopters, as well as by their ability to transport troops into combat. The Mi-25 is exceptionally well armed. It has a nose-mounted, four-barrelled 12.7mm gatling gun with 1400 rounds of ammunition and a high rate of fire. In addition, it can carry up to 4200kg (9240lb) of ordnance, which could include the UV-57-32 57mm unguided rocket pods, ATGMs, AAMs or even iron "dumb" bombs on six wing pylons. Internally, the Mi-25 can carry up to eight fully armed troops or four stretchers for casualty evacuation. India's Mi-25s have seen action along the Kashmiri border region in suppressing rebel activity, and are on constant standby in the event of war with neighbouring Pakistan. The Indian Hinds also saw action in the war against the Tamil Tigers in Sri Lanka. The missiles that the Mi-25 carries are capable of knocking out enemy armour at a range of more than 8km (5 miles), while the 57mm rockets can destroy soft targets at ranges in excess of 4km (2.5 miles).

SPECIFICATIONS

Manufacturer:	Mil Helicopter Factory
Mission:	attack, transport
Length:	18.5m (61ft)
Height:	6.5m (21ft)
Rotor Diameter:	17.3m (57ft)
Crew:	2
Propulsion:	2 x Isotov TV3-117
Horsepower:	4450 shaft horsepower
Maximum Speed:	335km/h (210mph)
Cruise Speed:	295km/h (185mph)
Vertical Rate of Climb:	750m/min (2460ft/min)
Range:	450km (281 miles)
Weight:	8500kg (18,700lb)
Date Deployed:	1976
Guns:	1 x 12.7mm chain gun
Missiles:	AT-6, 57mm rockets, AA-8 Aphid
Systems:	FLIR, RWR, laser-designator

MI-35 HIND E

The Mi-35 is the most recent export variation of the Russian-built Mi-24 Hind E. It is essentially the same highly effective aircraft, although there are some minor differences. The Mi-35 is armed with anti-tank missile systems for the engagement of moving armoured targets, weapon emplacements and slow-moving air targets. The aircraft retains its useful troop transport capability. The Mi-35 been exported to many countries including Angola, Bulgaria, Cuba, India, Iraq and North Korea. The two crew (pilot and weapons operator) are accommodated in tandem armoured cockpits with individual canopies and flat, bulletproof glass windscreens. The main cabin can accommodate eight fully equipped troops or four stretchers. The Mi-35 is fitted with a YakB four-barrelled, 12.7mm, built-in, flexibly mounted machine gun, which has a firing rate of 4000–4500 rounds per minute and a muzzle velocity of 860mps (2821fps). It is also armed with the Shturm ATGM system. Shturm (NATO designation AT-6 Spiral) is a short-range missile with semi-automatic radio command guidance. The 5.4kg (12lb) high-explosive fragmentation warhead is capable of penetrating up to 650mm (26in) of armour. Iraq is believed still to have some of these very capable Mi-35 attack and transport helicopters, but apparently hides them carefully.

SPECIFICATIONS

Manufacturer:	Mil Helicopter Factory
Mission:	attack, transport
Length:	18.5m (61ft)
Height:	6.5m (21ft)
Rotor Diameter:	17.3m (57ft)
Crew:	2
Propulsion:	2 x Isotov TV-3117
Horsepower:	4450 shaft horsepower
Maximum Speed:	335km/h (210mph)
Cruise Speed:	295km/h (185mph)
Vertical Rate of Climb:	750m/min (2460ft/min)
Range:	450km (281 miles)
Weight:	8500kg (18,700lb)
Date Deployed:	1976
Guns:	1 x 12.7mm chain gun
Missiles:	AT-6 Shturm, 57mm rockets
Systems:	FLIR, RWR, laser designator

PETEN

A s operated by the IAF, the AH-64A Peten is an older version of the renowned US-built Apache attack helicopter. The Longbow radar-equipped AH-64D is now being brought into Israeli service, but the most common version is the AH-64A. The firepower and capability of the Peten (meaning adder in Hebrew) is both well-known and feared. US-operated Apaches were highly effective during the 1991 Gulf War. The Apache entered Israeli service earlier than expected in 1990, after the original customer, ironically Kuwait, was invaded by Iraq. The design and avionics are identical to the US versions, with a few tweaks to adapt the aircraft to the Middle Eastern environment. Like the Israeli Tzefa, the Peten has seen a great deal of action in its first 12 years of service. It has been used in counter-terrorist operations against Palestinian and Lebanese guerrillas, scoring some remarkable successes in taking down senior terrorist leaders. Petens are fitted with 30mm automatic cannon, FFAR rockets and the fearsome Hellfire air-to-ground missile. The Longbow radar capability of the AH-64D version is somewhat redundant in the urban environments of the Palestinian territories, which makes the continued use of the less complex and technologically advanced AH-64A a sensible and cost-effective decision.

SPECIFICATIONS

Manufacturer:	*The Boeing Company*
Mission:	*multi-mission attack*
Length:	*17.7m (58ft)*
Height:	*4m (13ft)*
Rotor Diameter:	*14.6m (48ft)*
Crew:	*2*
Propulsion:	*2 x GE T700-701C*
Horsepower:	*1940 shaft horsepower*
Maximum Speed:	*365km/h (227mph)*
Cruise Speed:	*265km/h (165mph)*
Vertical Rate of Climb:	*450m/min (1475ft/min)*
Range:	*407km (253 miles)*
Weight:	*7800kg (17,000lb)*
Date Deployed:	*1990*
Guns:	*1 x 30mm automatic cannon*
Missiles:	*FFAR, Hellfire AGM*
Systems:	*TADS, PNVG, HADSS*

SAIFAN

The first two IAF Jet Rangers arrived in Israel in June 1971, and the type was nicknamed Saifan. Besides their regular role as light transports and VIP helicopters, the Saifans were also employed for casualty evacuation and pursuit of enemy forces. Other roles include directing Israeli ground fire against enemy positions and general reconnaissance. These helicopters have seen much of the action during Israel's recent conflicts, including the Yom Kippur War and the Palestinian *Intifada*. The Saifans also saw a great deal of action during the 1991 Gulf War. In an effort to drag Israel into the war, and thus destabilize the Allied coalition, Iraq launched Scud missiles at cities throughout Israel. There was widespread fear that these could contain chemical or biological agents capable of killing thousands of civilians. Every time Iraqi Scud missiles were launched against Israel, Saifans were scrambled to locate the point of impact, to determine whether the missile contained a chemical warhead and to direct SAR forces to the spot. The Saifan uses the same Bell 206 airframe as the US OH-58D Kiowa Warrior, and the Jet Ranger design is one of the most successful helicopters ever designed. It is in service in more than 30 countries around the world, in many guises.

SPECIFICATIONS

Manufacturer:	Bell Helicopter Textron
Mission:	light multi-purpose
Length:	9.5m (31ft)
Height:	2.9m (10ft)
Rotor Diameter:	10.2m (34ft)
Crew:	2
Propulsion:	1 x Allison 250-C20J
Horsepower:	420 shaft horsepower
Maximum Speed:	225km/h (140mph)
Cruise Speed:	216km/h (135mph)
Vertical Rate of Climb:	384m/min (1267ft/min)
Range:	748km (467 miles)
Weight:	742kg (1632lb)
Date Deployed:	1971
Guns:	none
Missiles:	none
Systems:	GPS, NBC agent detectors

TZEFA

Israel began a heavy defence procurement programme after the Yom Kippur War of October 1973, when the Israeli Defence Force (IDF) had initially failed to halt the Syrian armoured assault on the Golan Heights and the Egyptian crossing of the Suez Canal. Dense Arab air defences proved a deadly hindrance to Israeli Air Force (IAF) operations. Attack helicopters were seen as the solution, and this need provided the IAF with an incentive to procure attack helicopters of its own. The Cobra, or Tzefa as it is known in Hebrew, was selected to fulfil the Israeli procurement request and has been in service with the IDF since 1975. Given Israel's turbulent recent history, the Tzefa has probably seen more action than any other aircraft in Israeli service. It has been used in every theatre and at every level of conflict in which the IDF has been involved, including counter-terrorist operations against *Hizbullah*, as well as full-scale war in Lebanon. The first Tzefa attack took place on 9 May 1979, against a terrorist structure located inside a refugee camp near Tyre. The deadly aircraft continues to attack targets within Israeli and Palestinian territories. The use of Tzefa gunships in urban areas has been criticized in some sections of the international press but, in terrain where ground troops are easy targets for snipers, the helicopter is particularly effective.

SPECIFICATIONS

Manufacturer:	Bell Helicopter Textron
Mission:	fire-support, attack
Length:	13.8m (45ft)
Height:	4.4m (14ft)
Rotor Diameter:	14.6m (48ft)
Crew:	2
Propulsion:	1 x Lycoming T53-L-703
Horsepower:	1800 shaft horsepower
Maximum Speed:	290km/h (181mph)
Cruise Speed:	227km/h (141mph)
Vertical Rate of Climb:	494m/min (1630ft/min)
Range:	507km (316 miles)
Weight:	2939kg (6465lb)
Date Deployed:	1975
Guns:	1 x M197 20mm turreted cannon
Missiles:	TOW, 40mm grenade gun
Systems:	GPS, FLIR

YANSHUF

In 1997, Israel ordered its first newly built Black Hawks, or Yanshufs as they are known in Hebrew (meaning owl). These were 15 S-70As built under a foreign military sale agreement between the US Army and the IAF in a contract worth US$180 million to aircraft manufacturer Sikorsky. The S-70A-50 is similiar in configuration to that of the standard US Army UH-60L, but with Israeli modifications including locally built communications and ECM systems, as well as an HH-60G rescue hoist. Israeli versions of the Black Hawk include inflight refuelling probes and stub wings for 870l (191-gallon) drop tanks. In early 1999, the IAF began a major improvement programme involving the new UH-60Ls, equipping the 15 aircraft with the aforementioned inflight refuelling probes and shoulder-mounted fuel tanks that allow easy access to the cabin and the use of cabin mounted machine guns. Modifications were also made to the older UH-60As, including the installation of new communications, ECM, navigation, night vision and rescue systems. The summer of 2000 also saw the IAF apply a new desert camouflage scheme to several UH-60As in order to evaluate the possibility of making the normally all-black aircraft harder to detect. Although the results were said to be positive, this scheme appears no longer to be in use.

SPECIFICATIONS

Manufacturer:	Sikorsky Aircraft
Mission:	multi-mission utility
Length:	19.5m (64ft)
Height:	4.8m (16ft)
Rotor Diameter:	16.5m (53ft)
Crew:	3
Propulsion:	2 x GE T700-701C
Horsepower:	3300 shaft horsepower
Maximum Speed:	296km/h (184mph)
Cruise Speed:	257km/h (160mph)
Vertical Rate of Climb:	472m/min (1550ft/min)
Range:	584km (363 miles)
Weight:	5224kg (11,516lb)
Date Deployed:	1989
Guns:	2 x 7.62mm machine guns
Missiles:	none
Systems:	GPS, HH-60G rescue harness

AH-1J SEA COBRA

Built under licence by Fuji Heavy Industries, the AH-1 Sea Cobra joined the Japanese self defence forces in 1979, and 94 aircraft have been delivered since. The basic airframe design differs little from the US versions of the Cobra, but the powerplant and avionics are indigenous to Japan. The engine is manufactured by Kawasaki, and is less powerful than its US counterpart. The Japanese Cobra carries the same armament as the US version, namely the AGM-114 Hellfire missile system that provides heavy anti-armour capability for attack helicopters. The original Hellfire, such as those carried by Japanese AH-1J Cobras, are laser-guided, which means that the aircraft must remain in view of the target while the missile is in the air. This exposes the helicopter to enemy fire. The fourth-generation Longbow Hellfire is a fire-and-forget missile using a radar frequency seeker, which means the target can be acquired and engaged without the need to remain exposed. The Longbow version of the Hellfire AGMS is currently deployed only on the AH-64D Longbow Apaches, and provides a significant advantage over its predecessors. Japan's defence forces are now looking for a replacement for their ageing AH-1s, with the AH-64 Apache and the most modern Cobra heading the list.

SPECIFICATIONS

Manufacturer:	*Fuji Heavy Industries*
Mission:	*fire-support attack*
Length:	*13.9m (45ft)*
Height:	*4.4m (14ft)*
Rotor Diameter:	*14.6m (48ft)*
Crew:	*2*
Propulsion:	*2 x Kawasaki T53-K-703*
Horsepower:	*1800 shaft horsepower*
Maximum Speed:	*285km/h (178mph)*
Cruise Speed:	*227km/h (141mph)*
Vertical Rate of Climb:	*494m/min (1630ft/min)*
Range:	*507km (316 miles)*
Weight:	*2939kg (6465lb)*
Date Deployed:	*1990*
Guns:	*1 x M197 20mm turreted cannon*
Missiles:	*TOW, 40mm grenade gun, Hellfire*
Systems:	*GPS, FLIR*

CH-47J CHINOOK

The 1st Helicopter Brigade of the Japanese Ground Self-Defence Force (JGSDF) operates 32 CH-47J/JA Chinooks, manufactured locally by Kawasaki Heavy Industries (KHI) under licence from Boeing since its first delivery in 1988. The Japanese version of the Chinook resembles Britain's RAF version, with the exception of a different engine and slightly lower performance ratings. It is used for the same types of operation as in the US and Britain, generally in transportation, SAR and disaster relief operations. Kawasaki obtained two examples of the Chinook as pattern machines in 1986, and went on to build 54 more. The first five were assembled from kits supplied by Boeing. Some 40 of these CH-47Js were bought by the JGSDF, with another 16 obtained by the Japanese Air Self-Defence Force (JASDF). Later production of JGSDF Chinooks has been to CH-47JA standard. These machines are fitted with enlarged saddle tanks, nose radar, an AAQ-16 FLIR in a turret under the nose, and a partial glass cockpit. Though they are not generally configured for assault, the Japanese Chinooks could be easily pressed into frontline service if the situation called for it. Since Japan tends to take a backseat in international affairs, the CH-47J has not seen much action beyond Japanese territory, but is still invaluable to the JGSDF.

SPECIFICATIONS

Manufacturer:	Kawasaki Heavy Industries
Mission:	medium support
Length:	15.5m (51ft)
Height:	5.7m (19ft)
Rotor Diameter:	2 x 18.3m (60ft)
Crew:	3/4
Propulsion:	2 x T55-K-712
Horsepower:	4333 shaft horsepower
Maximum Speed:	274km/h (171mph)
Cruise Speed:	259km/h (161mph)
Vertical Rate of Climb:	561m/min (1841ft/min)
Range:	474km (300 miles)
Weight:	10,814kg (23,790lb)
Date Deployed:	1988
Guns:	none
Missiles:	none
Systems:	GPS, FLIR, PNVG

KV-107

Kawasaki's KV-107 is essentially a CH-46 Sea Knight as designed by Boeing. Following the signing of a license agreement in early 1962, Kawasaki Heavy Industries took up production of the V-107/II, as the aircraft was designated, under the model name KV-107/II. The first Kawasaki-built Sea Knight flew in May 1962. In 1965, the Japanese company signed a follow-on agreement with Boeing that allowed it to sell the helicopter on the world market. All commercial sales of the Sea Knight after that were from Kawasaki production. Thus, in many respects, the Sea Knights that operate around the world at present are essentially Japanese. The KV-107/II series was fitted with twin General Electric CT58-110-1 turboshaft engines or equivalent license-built Ishikawajima-Harima CT58-IHI-110-1 engines. Kawasaki built a number of variations of the KV-107, including a minesweeper for the Japanese Maritime Self Defence Force (JMSDF) and a troop transport version for the JGSDF. There was also a long-range SAR version, with additional fuel tanks, domed observation windows, four searchlights, a rescue hoist, plus enhanced navigation and communication electronics. Fourteen were built for the JASDF. The KV-107 helicopter has clearly been a considerable success for Kawasaki and the Japanese armed forces.

SPECIFICATIONS

Manufacturer:	Kawasaki Heavy Industries
Mission:	transport, SAR
Length:	13.4m (44ft)
Height:	5.1m (17ft)
Rotor Diameter:	2 x 15.2m (50ft)
Crew:	2
Propulsion:	2 x CT58-IHI-110-1
Horsepower:	2700 shaft horsepower
Maximum Speed:	270km/h (168mph)
Cruise Speed:	250km/h (156mph)
Vertical Rate of Climb:	500m/min (1650ft/min)
Range:	441km (275 miles)
Weight:	5248kg (11,545lb)
Date Deployed:	1962
Guns:	none
Missiles:	none
Systems:	GPS, searchlights, winch

OH-1 NINJA

Kawasaki designed and built the OH-1, nicknamed Ninja, as Japan's new indigenous battlefield scout helicopter. The initial prototype made its maiden flight on 6 August 1996. A total of four were delivered between May and August 1997. The JGSDF plans to purchase 180 to 200 of the OH-1s. Like similar types of light reconnaissance helicopters, the Ninja has tandem seating and stub wings for armament such as air-to-air missiles. The ducted tail rotor is of Fenestron type, in that the rotor is enclosed within the body of the tail. The design features a composite hinge-free rotor hub for high control responsibility. It also boasts damage-tolerant main rotor blades and an auto flight control system. The OH-1's targeting system is integrated, with FLIR, TV and laser ranging. The Ninja's shock-absorbing seat and crew protection armour are part of the integrated cockpit. KHI had been developing an all-composite, bearing-free helicopter main rotor system for more than 15 years. The bearing-free rotor system consists of a hub plate, torsion elements and the main rotor blades. The system is proving to be highly effective, and other variants of the OH-1 seem likely. Japan has a requirement to replace its 100 or so AH-1F Cobra attack helicopters, and one solution might be a Japanese design based on the OH-1 scout helicopter.

SPECIFICATIONS

Manufacturer:	Kawasaki Heavy Industries
Mission:	reconnaissance
Length:	12m (39ft)
Height:	3.8m (12ft)
Rotor Diameter:	11.5m (38ft)
Crew:	2
Propulsion:	2 x Mitsubishi XT1-10
Horsepower:	1700 shaft horsepower
Maximum Speed:	260km/h (162mph)
Cruise Speed:	200km/h (125mph)
Vertical Rate of Climb:	not available
Range:	550km (344mph)
Weight:	2500kg (5500lb)
Date Deployed:	1997
Guns:	none
Missiles:	air-to-air missiles
Systems:	GPS, FLIR, laser rangefinder

S-80M SEA DRAGON

The JMSDF S-80 Sea Dragon helicopter is used primarily for Airborne Mine Countermeasures (AMCM), with a secondary mission of shipboard delivery. The large aircraft is capable of carrying up to 55 troops or a 16-ton payload. It is also capable of towing a variety of minesweeping countermeasure systems, including the Mk 105 minesweeping sled, the AQS-14 side-scan sonar, and the Mk 103 mechanical minesweeping system. Since Japan is heavily reliant on imports for almost all of its energy and food, keeping open the vital shipping lanes is crucial. Thus the S-80 Sea Dragon, which is virtually identical to the US Navy's MH-53E, is charged with the task of keeping Japan's sea lanes free of mines, both during war and in peacetime. To achieve its goals, AMCM missions include minesweeping and ancillary spotting, mine neutralization, floating mine destruction, channel marking and surface towing of small craft and ships. For AMCM missions, the S-80 helicopter is operated by a crew of seven, comprising pilot, copilot, safety observer, port and starboard AMCM equipment handlers, and port and starboard ramp operators. The S-80 Sea Dragon can be refuelled inflight, as well as at the hover, which allows it to remain airborne for longer, thus extending its operational effectiveness.

SPECIFICATIONS

Manufacturer:	Sikorsky Aircraft
Mission:	heavy transport, minesweeping
Length:	30m (99ft)
Height:	8.5m (28ft)
Rotor Diameter:	24m (79ft)
Crew:	3/4
Propulsion:	3 x GE T64
Horsepower:	13,500 shaft horsepower
Maximum Speed:	315km/h (195mph)
Cruise Speed:	278km/h (172mph)
Vertical Rate of Climb:	420m/min (1386ft/min)
Range:	889km (550 miles)
Weight:	15,070kg (33,226lb)
Date Deployed:	1981
Guns:	2 x .50in machine guns
Missiles:	none
Systems:	GPS, FLIR, acoustic sensors, MAD

SH-60J SEAHAWK

Japan's self defence forces have contracted the SH-60J as a replacement for their ageing SH-3 Sea King ASW helicopter. Mitsubishi was selected to manufacture the SH-60J under licence from Sikorsky. While the basic airframe design is almost entirely from the original US-built S-70 Black Hawk (upon which the SH-60J is based), much of the helicopter is an indigenous Japanese design. The avionics are entirely Japanese, with the exception of the AN/APS-124 radar. The SH-60J first flew in Japanese service in August 1987. It is now in the process of replacing the elderly JMSDF-operated Sea Kings. Although used primarily as a patrol helicopter, operating onboard Japanese warships such as the Shirane or Haruna class ASW destroyers, the SH-60J can be configured to carry the necessary equipment to become an anti-submarine or anti-ship helicopter, in the same mould as the US Navy SH-60B Seahawk. While the SH-60J has never been deployed in war, it is on constant alert for unwanted intruders, with North Korean spy boats generally the prime suspects. The successful H-60 airframe from Sikorsky has shown itself to be the favourite for armed forces the world over. As a result, the Japanese Defence Agency (JDA) has ordered more of the MHI SH-60Js to replace its outdated HSS-2B aircraft.

SPECIFICATIONS

Manufacturer:	Mitsubishi Heavy Industries
Mission:	patrol
Length:	15.3m (50ft)
Height:	3.8m (13ft)
Rotor Diameter:	16.4m (54ft)
Crew:	3
Propulsion:	2 x GE T700-401C
Horsepower:	3400 shaft horsepower
Maximum Speed:	296km/h (184mph)
Cruise Speed:	250km/h (155mph)
Vertical Rate of Climb:	545m/min (1800ft/min)
Range:	833km (518 miles)
Weight:	6191kg (13,650lb)
Date Deployed:	1987
Guns:	none
Missiles:	none
Systems:	GPS, AN/APS-124 radar

SUPER LYNX

The latest generation of Lynx helicopters, the Super Lynx 300, took its maiden flight in June 2001. The first production version (for the Malaysian Navy) flew in May 2002. It incorporates an all-new glass cockpit with seven-colour active matrix liquid crystal displays (LCDs), new avionics, improved airframe, more powerful CTS800-4N engines (jointly developed by Rolls-Royce and the Honeywell partnership, LHTEC) with Full Authority Digital Electronic Control (FADEC). The new engines will operate more effectively in hot and humid conditions. A version of the Super Lynx 300, known as Future Lynx, is also to be developed to replace the British Army's Mk 7 and Mk 9 Lynx helicopters. The Lynx airframe is constructed of composite and light alloy. The non-retractable tricycle-type landing gear is designed for the helicopter to operate from small ships in high seas, and features oleo-pneumatic struts which absorb the shock of a 2m/sec (6ft/sec) descent rate. A hydraulically operated harpoon deck lock secures the helicopter to the deck. It is equipped with the Sea Skua, an all-weather anti-ship missile developed by Matra BAe Dynamics to provide medium- and long-range defence. Countries deploying the Sea Skua missile include Britain, Bahrain, Germany, South Korea, Brazil and Turkey. The Lynx carries four Sea Skua missiles.

SPECIFICATIONS

Manufacturer:	*Westland Helicopters*
Mission:	*naval multi-role*
Length:	*13.5m (44ft)*
Height:	*3.7m (12ft)*
Rotor Diameter:	*12.8m (42ft)*
Crew:	*2*
Propulsion:	*2 x Rolls-Royce/LHTEC CTS800-4N*
Horsepower:	*1800 shaft horsepower*
Maximum Speed:	*259km/h (161mph)*
Cruise Speed:	*225km/h (140mph)*
Vertical Rate of Climb:	*600m/min (1994ft/min)*
Range:	*590km (368 miles)*
Weight:	*3291kg (7240lb)*
Date Deployed:	*2002*
Guns:	*none*
Missiles:	*Sea Skua, depth charges, torpedoes*
Systems:	*Sea Spray radar, thermal imager*

KA-25 HORMONE

The deployment of the Polaris naval strategic nuclear missile system in the US acted as a catalyst that accelerated the development of aircraft-carrying ships in the former USSR. The KA-25 Hormone helicopter was developed to meet a Soviet Naval Air Force (SNAF) specification for an anti-submarine helicopter for ship- or shore-based use. The first KA-25 prototype flew in 1961. Designed by the world's leading pioneer of co-axial helicopters, Nikolai I. Kamov (1902–73), this Soviet AV-MF (naval aviation) ASW aircraft was assigned to the Soviet helicopter carrier *Moskva*. The KA-25 Hormone is powered by twin turbine engines – installed side-by-side above the cabin – which drive two three-bladed coaxial, contra-rotating rotors. The contra-rotating rotors eliminate the need for an anti-torque tail rotor. This makes a very compact design possible, with obvious benefits for shipboard operations. While still an effective aircraft, the Hormone was deployed more than 30 years ago and is now getting a little long in the tooth. One major drawback of the design is that the helicopter cannot hover or dip at night. This gives the Hormone's competitors a distinct advantage. However, the helicopter is still in widespread use, even though it has generally been superseded by more advanced and capable ASW aircraft.

SPECIFICATIONS

Manufacturer:	Kamov Company
Mission:	ASW, reconnaissance
Length:	9.8m (32 ft)
Height:	5.4m (17ft)
Rotor Diameter:	15.7m (52ft)
Crew:	2
Propulsion:	2 x Glushnekov GTD-3
Horsepower:	1700 shaft horsepower
Maximum Speed:	220km/h (137mph)
Cruise Speed:	195km/h (121mph)
Vertical Rate of Climb:	not available
Range:	400km (250 miles)
Weight:	7100kg (16,100lb)
Date Deployed:	1970
Guns:	none
Missiles:	E45-75A torpedo
Systems:	dipping sonar, 3 sonobuoys, MAD

KA-28 HELIX

NATO calls it the Helix, while its official designation is the Ka-28 naval anti-submarine helicopter, designed and manufactured by the Kamov Company in Russia. More than 60 Ka-27/28s are in service in Russia. The helicopters have also been exported to Cuba, India, Syria, Vietnam and the former Yugoslavia. The mission of these helicopters is to detect, track and destroy submerged submarines at depths of up to 500m (1640ft) and running at speeds up to 75km/h (47mph) at any time of the year and in all weather conditions. The Ka-28 has both day and night operations capability. It is equipped with a radar system for navigation and to detect surfaced submarines and responder beacons. The VGS-3 dipping sonar detects submarines, determines their coordinates and transfers the data in semi-automatic mode to data transmission equipment. The mission computer carries out automatic control, stabilization and guidance of the helicopter. The aircraft is also MAD-equipped and has an airborne receiver to detect and guide it towards sonobuoy radio transmissions. The export version Ka-28 also has an Identification Friend or Foe (IFF) system. The helicopter is armed with one homing torpedo, one torpedo rocket, 10 PLAB 250lb anti-submarine bombs and two OMAB marine marking bombs.

SPECIFICATIONS

Manufacturer:	Kamov Company
Mission:	ASW
Length:	12.2m (40ft)
Height:	5.4m (18ft)
Rotor Diameter:	15.9m (52ft)
Crew:	2
Propulsion:	2 x TV3-117V
Horsepower:	4000 shaft horsepower
Maximum Speed:	280km/h (175mph)
Cruise Speed:	240km/h (150mph)
Vertical Rate of Climb:	350m/min (1155ft/min)
Range:	450km (281 miles)
Weight:	5520kg (12,144lb)
Date Deployed:	1985
Guns:	2 x 7.62mm machine guns
Missiles:	torpedoes, PLAB, OMAB bombs
Systems:	MAD, VGS-3 dipping sonar

KA-29 HELIX B

Kamov's Ka-29 is the naval combat and transport helicopter version of the Ka-27. The mission of the aircraft is to land navy and infantry units from combatant ships and to ensure fire-support for seaborne assault troops. The helicopter can also ferry personnel and cargo from bases, and supply vessels to combatant ships. The Ka-29 is powered by two TV3-117V turboshaft engines. Its basic structure is very similar to that of the Ka-27 and Ka-28, and it can be re-equipped while on the assembly line. Transport and combat versions can be produced during assembly at the manufacturing plant, while the variants can also be changed in the field. The cargo cabin accommodates at least two tons of supplies or 16 armed troops. For casualty evacuation, it can carry four stretcher patients and seven seated wounded, with one medical attendant. According to the mission requirements, the helicopter can be armed with rockets, bombs and machine-gun pods mounted on the weapon pylons on both sides of the fuselage. Bombs and containers can be also arranged in the helicopter's torpedo bay. The helicopter is fitted with a 7.62mm flexibly mounted machine gun with 1800 rounds. A number of measures are taken to increase combat survivability, including armour protection. The Ka-29 has been in service with the Russian Armed Forces since 1985.

SPECIFICATIONS

Manufacturer:	Kamov Company
Mission:	naval combat, transport
Length:	12.2m (40ft)
Height:	5.4m (18ft)
Rotor Diameter:	15.9m (52ft)
Crew:	2
Propulsion:	2 x Isotov TV3-117V
Horsepower:	4000 shaft horsepower
Maximum Speed:	280km/h (175mph)
Cruise Speed:	240km/h (150mph)
Vertical Rate of Climb:	350m/min (1155ft/min)
Range:	450km (281 miles)
Weight:	5520kg (12,144lb)
Date Deployed:	1985
Guns:	1 x 7.62mm machine gun
Missiles:	rockets, bombs, torpedoes
Systems:	GPS

KA-32

The Ka-32 helicopter is intended for long-range detection of other aircraft, whether fixed or rotary wing. It is designed to find and track air targets at high or low altitudes and over water. It then transmits data automatically to the command posts. The helicopter can increase considerably the combat mission efficiency of all force elements by providing them with timely information about enemy air movements. Kamov's Ka-32 is developed from the basic Ka-27 ship-borne coaxial helicopter, taking its essential features and tailoring the equipment to suit its specialized mission. Under the transport cabin floor there is a compartment housing the support mechanism of a 6m (20ft)-span rotating antenna. The submarine search and attack equipment of the Ka-27 has been removed; instead, a radio-electronic suite is installed for radar target detection, target identification and transmission of the situation data to ship- and ground-based command posts. The radio-electronic package automatically controls the helicopter flight over the specified route in any climatic conditions. When the radio-electronic package is on, the antenna is extended and the navigator has selected the operational mode, all further operations are performed automatically without operator interference. Ka-32 helicopters are based aboard ships and at land locations.

SPECIFICATIONS

Manufacturer:	Kamov Company
Mission:	AEW
Length:	11.3m (37ft)
Height:	5.4m (18ft)
Rotor Diameter:	15.9m (52ft)
Crew:	2
Propulsion:	2 x Isotov TV3-117V
Horsepower:	4000 shaft horsepower
Maximum Speed:	280km/h (175mph)
Cruise Speed:	235km/h (146mph)
Vertical Rate of Climb:	924m/min (3050ft/min)
Range:	460km (287 miles)
Weight:	5520kg (12,170lb)
Date Deployed:	1995
Guns:	1 x 7.62mm machine gun
Missiles:	AT-6, rockets
Systems:	E-801 OKO 360-degree radar

KA-50 HOKUM

The Ka-50 Hokum, nicknamed Werewolf or Black Shark, is a powerful, state-of-the-art battle helicopter in limited service with the Russian Air Force. There are two versions. The Ka-50 Hokum is a single-seat, close-support aircraft and is competing to fulfil the Russian Army Aviation requirement for a night-capable anti-tank helicopter, a replacement for the 25-year-old Mi-24. The helicopter has a number of special features, including its single seat to improve combat and flight characteristics and reduce operational costs. It was designed for remote operations, with no need of ground maintenance facilities for two weeks at a time. The fully armoured pilot's cabin can withstand 23mm gunfire. The pilot ejection system functions at any height and allows successful ejection at low altitude and maximum speed. A typical mix for targeting armour formations is 12x AT-16 ATGMs, 500 x 30mm cannon rounds and two 20-round pods of 80mm FFAR. It also carries guided air-to-air missiles. The Hokum's most remarkable feature is a remote targeting system that can facilitate an effective attack from a distance that rules out direct visual contact with the target. However, as with much of the recent Russian military procurement programme, the Ka-50 development has suffered due to lack of funds and may never see widespread service.

SPECIFICATIONS

Manufacturer:	Kamov Company
Mission:	attack
Length:	15m (50ft)
Height:	4.9m (16ft)
Rotor Diameter:	14.5m (48ft)
Crew:	1
Propulsion:	2 x Klimov TV3
Horsepower:	4000 shaft horsepower
Maximum Speed:	340km/h (212mph)
Cruise Speed:	290km/h (181mph)
Vertical Rate of Climb:	600m/min (1980ft/min)
Range:	460km (290 miles)
Weight:	7692kg (16,922lb)
Date Deployed:	2000
Guns:	1 x 2A42 30mm cannon
Missiles:	AT-16, 80mm rockets, AA-11
Systems:	FLIR, TV or thermal sight, PNVG

KA-52 ALLIGATOR

Nicknamed Alligator, the Ka-52 is the second version of the Ka-50 in limited service with the Russian Air Force. It is a twin-seat, close-support helicopter that is also used as a trainer for the single-seat Ka-50. The helicopter has two pilots who sit side-by-side rather than one behind the other, and is therefore heavier than its single-seat counterpart. Performance is marginally reduced as a result. The Ka-52 is intended for a wide range of combat tasks in daytime and night conditions. It can operate in most weather conditions and has the same capabilities as the Ka-50. The Ka-52 helicopter differs through a wider nose part and the side-by-side, twin-seat crew cockpit. Both pilots have full control of the helicopter without any limitations. Numerous weapon options are achieved by arranging a movable, high-speed firing gun starboard of the helicopter, and by six external wing stores with different combinations of anti-tank missiles, rockets, air-to-air missiles and bombs. The Alligator is comparable with the Werewolf helicopter in terms of weaponry, if not weight, and is a match for most existing combat helicopters. However, as with the Ka-50, there is serious doubt about whether the Ka-52 will see any kind of widespread deployment within Russia's armed forces for reasons of cost and inefficiency in the post-Soviet era.

SPECIFICATIONS

Manufacturer:	Kamov Company
Mission:	attack
Length:	15m (50ft)
Height:	4.6m (15ft)
Rotor Diameter:	14.5m (48ft)
Crew:	2
Propulsion:	2 x Klimov TV3
Horsepower:	4000 shaft horsepower
Maximum Speed:	330km/h (206mph)
Cruise Speed:	279km/h (174mph)
Vertical Rate of Climb:	600m/min (1980ft/min)
Range:	460km (290 miles)
Weight:	7930kg (17,446lb)
Date Deployed:	2000
Guns:	1 x 2A42 30mm cannon
Missiles:	AT-16, 80mm rockets, AA-11
Systems:	FLIR, TV or thermal sight, PNVG

KA-60 KASATKA

Known as the Killer Whale, the Ka-60 Kasatka is a medium-weight transport helicopter developed by Kamov. Aircraft from Kamov are best known for their coaxial contra-rotating rotor design, but the Ka-60 has a single four-bladed main rotor with an anti-torque tail rotor. The Ka-60 is intended as a replacement for the outmoded Mi-8 in the Russian military, offering a 60 percent saving in fuel consumption as well as far superior reliability and maintainability. It is to fulfil a wide variety of roles, from training and troop transport to all-weather reconnaissance and target designation for attack helicopters. The Ka-60 is designed for carrying troops, weapons and ammunition to the battlefield, evacuation of casualties and cargo transport using the external hook. Kamov first unveiled the Ka-60 helicopter in 1997, and its first flight took place in 1998. The helicopter went on international display at the MAKS 1999 show held in Moscow. Kamov has announced that production will start in 2003 at the RSK MiG Lukhovitsky machine-building plant near Moscow. As well as the Ka-60 transport, Kamov has developed a civilian utility variant, the Ka-62. More so than other Russian developments in helicopter design, the Ka-60 has a real chance of success. Away from Russia's sphere of influence, though, it faces stiff opposition from other makers.

SPECIFICATIONS

Manufacturer:	Kamov Company
Mission:	medium transport
Length:	13.5m (45ft)
Height:	3.8m (13ft)
Rotor Diameter:	13.5m (45ft)
Crew:	2
Propulsion:	2 x RD-600V
Horsepower:	2400 shaft horsepower
Maximum Speed:	300km/h (187mph)
Cruise Speed:	275km/h (171mph)
Vertical Rate of Climb:	624m/min (2059ft/min)
Range:	625km (390 miles)
Weight:	6000kg (13,200lb)
Date Deployed:	2000
Guns:	2x 7.62mm machine gun
Missiles:	80mm rockets
Systems:	GPS, Arbalet radar

MI-2 HOPLITE

The elderly Mi-2 Hoplite provides transport and fire-support services. The helicopter can conduct reconnaissance, re-supply guerrillas and provide close air support with 57mm rockets. It can also have a smoke generator mounted to provide a wide-area smokescreen in front of ground units, screening their movements. Additional missions include direct air support, anti-tank, armed reconnaissance, transport, medevac, airborne command post, mine-laying and training. Although the Mi-2 Hoplite was developed by the Mil bureau in the former Soviet Union, the aircraft was produced exclusively in Poland by the WSK-PZL Swidnik aircraft factory. Several thousand of these aircraft were built, and they remained in production until 1985. The cabin door is hinged rather than sliding, which can limit operations. There is no armour protection for the cockpit or cabin. Ammunition storage is in the aircraft cabin, so combat load varies by mission. Some Mi-2s currently employ fuselage-mounted weapon racks rather than the standard 23mm fuselage-mounted cannon. Other variants employ the cannon. Although production has now ceased, the Mi-2 Hoplite still operates successfully in more than 20 countries, though generally in more of a paramilitary or law enforcement role, rather than in a frontline military capacity.

SPECIFICATIONS

Manufacturer:	*Mil/PZL Swidnik*
Mission:	*transport, cargo, reconnaissance*
Length:	*11.9m (39ft)*
Height:	*3.7m (12ft)*
Rotor Diameter:	*14.6m (47ft)*
Crew:	*1/2*
Propulsion:	*2 x PZL GTD-350*
Horsepower:	*760 shaft horsepower*
Maximum Speed:	*220km/h (137mph)*
Cruise Speed:	*194km/h (121mph)*
Vertical Rate of Climb:	*270m/min (891ft/min)*
Range:	*580km (362 miles)*
Weight:	*2372kg (5218lb)*
Date Deployed:	*1965*
Guns:	*23mm cannon*
Missiles:	*AT-3, SA-7, 57mm rockets*
Systems:	*GPS, basic flight systems*

MI-8 HIP

The Mi-8 Hip is a highly successful multi-role transport helicopter capable of carrying troops or supplies as well as conducting armed attacks with rockets and guns. Introduced as a replacement for the Mi-4 Hound, it is often used to re-supply guerrillas, insert troops or provide close air support to attacking units. Designed as a transport helicopter, the Mi-8 proved to be a versatile machine capable of carrying large cargo sizes weighing up to three tons. If required, it can become both combat, rescue and artillery observation helicopter, accommodating three crew. The first Mi-8 flew in January 1960, and by 1985 more than 1500 had been built. The success of this helicopter has seen it become the base design for the export version Mi-17 and the naval Mi-14. It has been exported to dozens of countries and seen plenty of combat. The survivability features of the Mi-8 include crew cabin armour plating, explosive-resistant foam filling in the fuel tanks, a fire-fighting system, plus duplicated and back-up hydraulics, power systems and main control circuits. An SAR version was developed from the military transport helicopter. In rescue missions, the helicopter crew drop radio-beacons to mark the distress area and deliver rescue teams to aid and recover the casualties.

SPECIFICATIONS

Manufacturer:	Mil Helicopter Factory
Mission:	armed transport
Length:	18.4m (61ft)
Height:	5.7m (19ft)
Rotor Diameter:	21.3m (70ft)
Crew:	3
Propulsion:	2 x Isotov TV3-117
Horsepower:	3500 shaft horsepower
Maximum Speed:	240km/h (150mph)
Cruise Speed:	225km/h (140mph)
Vertical Rate of Climb:	540m/min (1782ft/min)
Range:	495km (309 miles)
Weight:	7200kg (15,840lb)
Date Deployed:	1981
Guns:	2 x 7.62mm machine guns
Missiles:	AT-2, AT-3, 57mm rockets
Systems:	autopilot, PNVG, infrared jammer

MI-14 HAZE

A shore-based naval version of the Mi-8 Hip, the Mi-14 Haze has a boat-shaped bottom and fully retractable undercarriage, enabling it to land on water. The aircraft can be fitted with ASW equipment, with a radome under the nose and MAD mounted under the tail boom. It is equally happy in SAR or mine-sweeping roles. In addition to its multi-role capability, the Mi-14 features high flight performance, boasting a maximum 1135km (709 mile) range. Currently, its only real competitor is the Eurocopter AS 332L1 Super Puma. When functioning in its SAR guise, the Mi-14 Haze can land on water, drop up to 20 liferafts overboard and accommodate at least 20 survivors. The Haze is similar to the Mi-8 in terms of the fuselage, but with the addition of the boat hull. The engines are the same Isotov turboshafts as those fitted to the Mi-24 Hind gunship series. Rescue versions do not typically carry any armament, but do have a 500kg (1102lb) capacity winch above the side door. The Mi-14PL is the ASW version, while the minesweeper is designated Mi-14BT and the Mi-14PS is the SAR derivative. The Haze has been exported very successfully by Russia, and is currently operated by Bulgaria, Cuba, Ethiopia, North Korea, Poland, Romania, Syria and the former Yugoslavia.

SPECIFICATIONS

Manufacturer:	*Mil Helicopter Factory*
Mission:	*SAR, ASW*
Length:	*25.3m (83ft)*
Height:	*6.9m (22ft)*
Rotor Diameter:	*21.3m (70ft)*
Crew:	*3*
Propulsion:	*2 x Isotov TV3-117*
Horsepower:	*3354 shaft horsepower*
Maximum Speed:	*230km/h (143mph)*
Cruise Speed:	*215km/h (134mph)*
Vertical Rate of Climb:	*not available*
Range:	*1135km (709 miles)*
Weight:	*9000kg (19,800lb)*
Date Deployed:	*not available*
Guns:	*none*
Missiles:	*E45-75A torpedo, depth charges*
Systems:	*MAD, dipping sonar, sonobuoys*

MI-17 HIP H

The Mi-17 is a multi-role helicopter derivative of the Russian Mi-8 Hip, and can be used to re-supply or insert troop detachments. It can also be very heavily armed with an extensive array of rockets, missiles and guns. It is often used by air assault infantry forces to attack the point of penetration, reinforce units in contact or disrupt counterattacks. Additional missions include attack, direct air support, electronic warfare, AEW, medevac, SAR and minelaying. The Mi-17 is manufactured at the Kazan Helicopter Production Association for export. The Russian armed forces call it Mi-8MT. The Mi-17 can be recognized because it has the tail rotor at the starboard side, instead of at the port side. It is capable of carrying cargo in the cabin with half-open or removed doors, plus external loads or passengers. Up to 30 armed troops and up to 20 wounded can also be accommodated. The aircraft can be used for in-flight unloading of special cargoes. The Mi-17 is provided with missiles, bombs, small arms and cannon. It may be equipped with long-range communication equipment and radar. In addition, it can carry equipment with phased-array antennae for suppression of enemy electronic attack and neutralization of air defence facilities such as surface-to-air-missile (SAM) sites.

SPECIFICATIONS

Manufacturer:	*Mil/Kazan*
Mission:	*armed multi-role*
Length:	*18.4m (61ft)*
Height:	*5.7m (19ft)*
Rotor Diameter:	*21.3m (70ft)*
Crew:	*3*
Propulsion:	*2 x Isotov TV3-117MT*
Horsepower:	*4000 shaft horsepower*
Maximum Speed:	*250km/h (156mph)*
Cruise Speed:	*240km/h (150mph)*
Vertical Rate of Climb:	*540m/min (1782ft/min)*
Range:	*495km (309 miles)*
Weight:	*7200kg (15,840lb)*
Date Deployed:	*1981*
Guns:	*2 x 7.62mm machine guns*
Missiles:	*rockets, missiles, bombs*
Systems:	*autopilot, PNVG, infrared jammer*

MI-24 HIND

Feared on the battlefield, the Mi-24 Hind is a versatile attack helicopter with transport capabilities. Developed around the Mi-8 Hip's propulsion system, it was the first helicopter to enter service with the Russian Air Force as an assault transport and gunship. Other missions include direct air support, anti-tank, armed escort and air combat. The helicopter was used extensively in the Russia/Afghanistan war, becoming the signature weapon of the conflict. The Mi-24 is a close counterpart to the US Apache but, unlike this and other Western attack helicopters, it is also capable of transporting up to eight troops. Able to carry different types of ammunition, a typical armament make-up would be eight AT-6 ATGMs, 750x 30mm rounds, plus two 57mm rocket pods. The Hind can store additional ammunition in the cargo compartment in lieu of troops. Armoured cockpits and a titanium rotor head are able to withstand 20mm cannon hits. Every aircraft has an overpressurization system for operation in a nuclear, bacteriological or chemical (NBC) environment. Because of problems with their flight characteristics, which can leave them temporarily vulnerable to more nimble aircraft, they usually attack in pairs or groups from various directions. This negates any weakness from which a single aircraft might suffer.

SPECIFICATIONS

Manufacturer:	Mil Helicopter Factory
Mission:	attack, transport
Length:	18.5m (61ft)
Height:	6.5m (21ft)
Rotor Diameter:	17.3m (57ft)
Crew:	2
Propulsion:	2 x Isotov TV3-117
Horsepower:	4450 shaft horsepower
Maximum Speed:	335km/h (210mph)
Cruise Speed:	295km/h (185mph)
Vertical Rate of Climb:	750m/min (2460ft/min)
Range:	495km (309 miles)
Weight:	8500kg (18,700lb)
Date Deployed:	1976
Guns:	1 x 12.7mm chain gun
Missiles:	AT-6, 57mm rockets, AA-8 Aphid
Systems:	FLIR, RWR, laser designator

MI-26 HALO

The Mi-26 Halo is the heaviest and most powerful helicopter in the world, designed to carry large-size cargoes weighing up to 20.3 tonnes (20 tons). It is the result of an early 1970s specification for a transport helicopter whose empty weight, without fuel, was not to exceed half of its maximum take-off weight. It can be used for construction projects ranging from bridges to power transmission lines. The combination of high load-carrying capacity and high cruise speed makes the use of the helicopter economically efficient. The Halo has no armament. The load and lift capabilities of the aircraft are comparable to those of the US C-130 Hercules transport aircraft. The Halo has a closed-circuit television (CCTV) system to observe positioning over a sling load, and to monitor load operations. The Mi-26 has some variants including a medevac version, a freight transporter and a fuel tanker. It is an awesome aircraft, and has seen action all over the world, taking part in Russia's war in Afghanistan. It has been exported to many other nations, including India and most of the former Soviet republics. It is capable of carrying 100 troops as well as armoured vehicles. It is still in operation and, on occasion, is hired by Western nations that require a heavy-lift helicopter to transport equipment into areas that a normal fixed-wing aircraft cannot reach.

SPECIFICATIONS

Manufacturer:	*Mil Helicopter Factory*
Mission:	*heavy transport*
Length:	*33.5m (110ft)*
Height:	*8.1m (26ft)*
Rotor Diameter:	*32m (105ft)*
Crew:	*5*
Propulsion:	*2 x Lotarev D-136*
Horsepower:	*22,300 shaft horsepower*
Maximum Speed:	*295km/h (184mph)*
Cruise Speed:	*255km/h (159mph)*
Vertical Rate of Climb:	*not available*
Range:	*800km (500 miles)*
Weight:	*28,200kg (62,040lb)*
Date Deployed:	*1983*
Guns:	*none*
Missiles:	*none*
Systems:	*internal auto-loading system*

MI-28 HAVOC

Known by the NATO codename Havoc, the Mi-28 combat helicopter is a rival to the Ka-50 Hokum, or Werewolf. The new Mil design is based on the conventional pod and boom configuration with a tail rotor. An innovative design of all-plastic rotor blades, which can survive hits from 30mm cannon shells, has been installed on the Night Havoc Mi-28N version. Engines are two TV3-117 turboshafts, providing high speed and reasonable range. Energy-absorbing landing gear and seats protect the crew in a crash landing or in a low-altitude vertical fall. The two crew members are able to survive a vertical fall of up to 12m/sec (39ft/sec). The Mi-28N Night Havoc is armed with Shturm and Ataka anti-tank missiles. The former weapon is radio command guided, while the latter has a radar guidance system and considerably longer range. Up to 16 anti-tank missiles can be mounted on the aircraft. The helicopter can also carry four containers each with 20x 80mm unguided rockets or with five 122mm rockets. The Havoc is equipped with a turreted 2A42 30mm cannon. The pilot uses a helmet-mounted target designator, which allocates the target to the navigator's surveillance and fire control system. The navigator/weapons officer is then able to deploy guided weapons or the gun against the target.

SPECIFICATIONS

Manufacturer:	*Mil Helicopter Factory*
Mission:	*attack*
Length:	*17m (56ft)*
Height:	*3.8m (13ft)*
Rotor Diameter:	*17.2m (57ft)*
Crew:	*2*
Propulsion:	*2 x Isotov TV3-117VMA*
Horsepower:	*4000 shaft horsepower*
Maximum Speed:	*324km/h (202mph)*
Cruise Speed:	*265km/h (165mph)*
Vertical Rate of Climb:	*810m/min (2675ft/min)*
Range:	*460km (287 miles)*
Weight:	*7890kg (17,358lb)*
Date Deployed:	*2001*
Guns:	*1 x 2A42 30mm cannon*
Missiles:	*Shturm, Ataka*
Systems:	*GPS, FLIR, terrain-following radar*

AH-2 ROOIVALK

The Rooivalk is a latest-generation attack helicopter from Denel Aviation of South Africa. It has completed the development, test and evaluation phase and entered full-scale production. The South African Air Force (SAAF) has ordered 16 Rooivalk AH-2s for two squadrons, the first of which entered service in July 1999. The Rooivalk has a crash-resistant structure and is designed for stealth with low radar, visual, infrared and acoustic signatures. It carries a comprehensive range of weaponry selected for the mission requirement, ranging from anti-armour and anti-helicopter missions to ground suppression and ferry duties. The aircraft can engage multiple targets at short and long range, utilizing the nose-mounted cannon and a range of underwing-mounted munitions. Denel is developing the Mokopa anti-tank missile for the Rooivalk. Mokopa has either a semi-active laser or millimetre wave radar seeker head, and is equipped with a tandem warhead. Range is more than 8km (5 miles). Rooivalk can also fire Hellfire or HOT 3 missiles, and can carry four air-to-air missiles such as the Kentron V3C Darter or MBDA Mistral. The Rooivalk's electronic warfare suite is the fully integrated Helicopter Electronic Warfare Self-Protection Suite (HEWSS), incorporating radar warning, laser warning and countermeasures.

SPECIFICATIONS

Manufacturer:	*Denel Aviation*
Mission:	*attack*
Length:	*18.7m (62ft)*
Height:	*5.1m (17ft)*
Rotor Diameter:	*15.6m (51ft)*
Crew:	*2*
Propulsion:	*2 x GTE Makila 1K2*
Horsepower:	*not available*
Maximum Speed:	*371km/h (231mph)*
Cruise Speed:	*278km/h (173mph)*
Vertical Rate of Climb:	*798m/min (2633ft/min)*
Range:	*700km (438 miles)*
Weight:	*5730kg (12,606lb)*
Date Deployed:	*1999*
Guns:	*1 x 20mm cannon*
Missiles:	*ATM Mokopa, Hellfire, FFAR*
Systems:	*GPS, FLIR, HUD*

DENEL ORYX

Atlas Denel's Oryx helicopter is the South African National Defence Force version of the SA 330B Puma. It shares many of the same characteristics, but has had a number of modifications made to it in order to improve performance in South Africa's more demanding climate. Such improvements include filters for the air intakes which prevent sand and dust getting into the engines. Also, the aircraft has been modified to make operating in the heat of South Africa's inner territories more practical. In its operational roles, the Oryx can carry up to 20 fully armed combat troops, or six stretchers for medical evacuation. The South African armed forces have embarked on a modernization drive to improve their fighting abilities, and integration of the Oryx helicopter into troop manoeuvre and deployment has been central to this process. Indeed, South Africa recently took part in a joint training exercise with the US where Oryx helicopters were used to evacuate dozens of casualties to a mobile field hospital. The Oryx replaced the older Eurocopter Puma that the air force had been using since the 1970s. Though the new Oryx is essentially a Eurocopter AS 332 Super Puma, the extensive modifications made to the basic design by the two South African companies Atlas and Denel make it a very different beast to its European counterparts.

SPECIFICATIONS

Manufacturer:	Atlas Denel
Mission:	utility transport
Length:	15.5m (51ft)
Height:	4.9m (16ft)
Rotor Diameter:	15m (49ft)
Crew:	2
Propulsion:	2 x Turbomeca Makila
Horsepower:	3500 shaft horsepower
Maximum Speed:	271km/h (169mph)
Cruise Speed:	258km/h (161mph)
Vertical Rate of Climb:	420m/min (1386ft/min)
Range:	850km (531 miles)
Weight:	4370kg (9614lb)
Date Deployed:	1992
Guns:	2 x 7.62 machine guns
Missiles:	none
Systems:	GPS

AH-1W SUPER COBRA

The Bell AH-1W Super Cobra is a day/night marginal-weather US Marine Corps (USMC) attack helicopter that provides en-route escort for assault helicopters and their embarked forces. The AH-1W is a two-crew, tandem-seat, twin-engine helicopter capable of land- or sea-based operations. It provides fire support and fire support coordination to the landing force during amphibious assaults and subsequent operations ashore. The original AH-1 Cobra was conceived and built during the 1960s, and saw action in the Vietnam War. It has gone through a number of changes over the years, with the newest incarnation, the AH-1Z, currently in development. It is a testament to the vision of the original design concept that the twenty-first century model bears more than a passing resemblance to its less technologically advanced predecessors, given the pace of development and fierce competition in the attack helicopter marketplace. While the AH-1 Cobra is in service with armed forces the world over in its various guises, the Super Cobra represents the pinnacle of AH-1 development. This helicopter has served with great distinction in many of the late twentieth century's conflicts, including the Gulf War, the Balkans and most recently in Afghanistan. The Super Cobra's potent arsenal of advanced weaponry gives it a distinct advantage on the modern battlefield.

SPECIFICATIONS

Manufacturer:	Bell Helicopter Textron
Mission:	close-support attack
Length:	13.9m (45ft)
Height:	4.4m (14ft)
Rotor Diameter:	14.6m (48ft)
Crew:	2
Propulsion:	2 x GE T700-401
Horsepower:	2082 shaft horsepower
Maximum Speed:	313km/h (195mph)
Cruise Speed:	278km/h (173mph)
Vertical Rate of Climb:	583m/min (1925ft/min)
Range:	470km (294 miles)
Weight:	4634kg (10,194lb)
Date Deployed:	1986
Guns:	1 x M-197 20mm turreted cannon
Missiles:	Hellfire, Sidewinder, Sidearm
Systems:	Kollsman night target system

AH-64D APACHE

Boeing's (McDonnell Douglas) AH-64 Apache is the US Army's primary attack helicopter. It is a fast, quick-reacting, airborne weapon system. The Apache is designed to fight and survive during the day, night and in adverse weather conditions. The principal mission is the destruction of high-value targets with the Hellfire missile. It is also capable of employing a 30mm M230 chain gun and Hydra 70mm (2.75in) rockets that are effective against a wide variety of targets. The Apache has a full range of aircraft survivability equipment, and has the ability to withstand hits in critical areas from rounds of up to 23mm. The AH-64D variation of the Apache, introduced in 1998, is the latest addition and incorporates the state-of-the-art Longbow radar system. This enables it to locate, designate and prioritize battlefield targets, disseminate the information to other aircraft in the area, and then initiate a precision attack. These targets can be engaged and destroyed from a distance of up to 8km (5 miles). The AH-64D further enhances the Apache's fearsome reputation with a claimed 400 percent increase in target destruction and a 720 percent increase in survivability. All the existing AH-64A variants of the Apache are to be upgraded to AH-64D Longbow standards.

SPECIFICATIONS

Manufacturer:	*The Boeing Company*
Mission:	*multi-mission attack*
Length:	*17.7m (58ft)*
Height:	*4m (13ft)*
Rotor Diameter:	*14.6 (48ft)*
Crew:	*2*
Propulsion:	*2 x GE T700-701C*
Horsepower:	*1940 shaft horsepower*
Maximum Speed:	*365km/h (227mph)*
Cruise Speed:	*265km/h (165mph)*
Vertical Rate of Climb:	*450m/min (1475ft/min)*
Range:	*407km (253 miles)*
Weight:	*7800kg (17,000lb)*
Date Deployed:	*1998*
Guns:	*1 x M230 30mm chain gun*
Missiles:	*FFAR, Hellfire, Sidearm, AIM-9*
Systems:	*TADS/PNVG, Longbow radar*

BA609

A trial of the BA609 tilt-rotor aircraft is currently taking place with the United States Coast Guard (USCG), leading to a possible introduction into the existing helicopter fleet as a potential replacement for established aircraft types. The BA609 uses the same type of technology employed on the V-22 Osprey. In fact, much of the research and development that went into the Osprey was evaluated during the creation of the BA609, but it is a completely new design. As aviation companies look to expand their customer bases beyond that of either purely the military or commercial businesses, the BA609 is an aircraft that can cross the boundaries. Thus the USCG has the aircraft on trial, while other military organizations around the world have placed small orders to test and evaluate the tilt-rotor concept. The advantages of an aircraft that can take off or land vertically, and then utilize the straight-line speed of a fixed-wing aircraft, are obvious, and already demonstrated by the successful Harrier jet fighter-bomber. However, it is only with technological developments in recent years that a tilt-rotor aircraft has become a viable proposition. Should the trials of the BA609 prove successful, then it will not only be an excellent addition to the USCG fleet but will probably find other military applications.

SPECIFICATIONS

Manufacturer:	Agusta/Bell Helicopter Textron
Mission:	SAR
Length:	13.3m (44ft)
Height:	4.5m (15ft)
Rotor Diameter:	2 x 7.9m (26ft)
Crew:	2
Propulsion:	2 x P & W Canada PT6C
Horsepower:	3800 shaft horsepower
Maximum Speed:	510km/h (318mph)
Cruise Speed:	465km/h (290mph)
Vertical Rate of Climb:	not available
Range:	1500km (937 miles)
Weight:	4765kg (10,483lb)
Date Deployed:	2002
Guns:	none
Missiles:	none
Systems:	GPS

CH-46E SEA KNIGHT

The CH-46E Sea Knight is an ageing yet integral part of the USMC assault forces. Troop assault is the primary function of this distinctive twin-rotor helicopter, and the movement of supplies and equipment is secondary. Additional tasks can be combat and assault support for evacuation and other maritime special operations, over-water SAR augmentation, support for mobile forward refuelling and re-arming points or aeromedical evacuation of casualties from the field to suitable medical facilities. The CH-46 Sea Knight was first procured in 1964 to meet the medium-lift requirements of the USMC in Vietnam, but its transition from the design phase to operations was far from smooth. A great many aircraft were lost during development, and troops were initially sceptical about it. However, it quickly won over its doubters and has served with great success in all combat and peacetime environments. It is nearing the end of its operational life, as normal airframe operational and attrition rates have taken the aircraft to the point where a medium-lift replacement is required. The V-22 Osprey has been designated as its replacement, and there is a certain irony in the fact that the USMC is as sceptical about the new aircraft as it was 40 years ago about the Sea Knight.

SPECIFICATIONS

Manufacturer:	*The Boeing Company*
Mission:	*medium-lift assault*
Length:	*13.9m (45ft)*
Height:	*5m (16ft)*
Rotor Diameter:	*2 x 15.2m (50ft)*
Crew:	*4*
Propulsion:	*2 x GE T58*
Horsepower:	*3600 shaft horsepower*
Maximum Speed:	*267km/h (166mph)*
Cruise Speed:	*222km/h (138mph)*
Vertical Rate of Climb:	*522m/min (1715ft/min)*
Range:	*1111km (690 miles)*
Weight:	*7257kg (16,000lb)*
Date Deployed:	*1978*
Guns:	*2 x 7.62mm M-60 machine guns*
Missiles:	*none*
Systems:	*PNVG*

CH-47D CHINOOK

The CH-47 Chinook is a tandem-rotored, twin-engined, medium-lift helicopter. It has a crew of four, comprising a pilot, a navigator and two crewmen. It is capable of carrying 45 fully equipped troops or a variety of heavy loads up to approximately 10.1 tonnes (10 tons). It is a rugged and reliable aircraft, and has been at the forefront of US military operations for several decades. It is in service with a number of armed forces around the world, including Britain. During the Falklands War it is reported that, at one stage, 80 fully equipped troops were carried in one lift by an RAF Chinook. Indeed, during a Gulf War mission, a single US Chinook carried 110 Iraqi prisoners of war. The Chinook has a famous load-carrying capability, able to transport a wide range of equipment. Its primary mission is moving artillery, ammunition, personnel and supplies, but it also performs rescue, aeromedical, parachuting, aircraft recovery and special operations missions. The image of a Chinook with an artillery piece or jeep underslung is one of the most iconic in modern warfare. Despite the age of the design, the Chinook has many years left in it. The first-rate military powers have recently finished updating their Chinooks to the newest CH-47D model, and the US will be upgrading once more to the Improved Cargo Helicopter (ICH) model by 2004.

SPECIFICATIONS

Manufacturer:	The Boeing Company
Mission:	medium support
Length:	15.5m (51ft)
Height:	5.7m (19ft)
Rotor Diameter:	2 x 18.3m (60ft)
Crew:	4
Propulsion:	2 x Textron Lycoming T55-L-712
Horsepower:	7500 shaft horsepower
Maximum Speed:	269km/h (167mph)
Cruise Speed:	265km/h (165mph)
Vertical Rate of Climb:	561m/min (1841ft/min)
Range:	600km (375 miles)
Weight:	10,814kg (23,790lb)
Date Deployed:	1987
Guns:	3 x 7.62mm M-60 machine guns
Missiles:	none
Systems:	GPS, PNVG

CH-53E SEA STALLION

Sea Stallions are the US Navy's heavy-lift helicopters, capable of carrying up to 16,330kg (36,000lb), including artillery pieces and light armour. The machines can also retrieve downed aircraft, including another CH-53E. This massive lifting power has proved invaluable to the US Navy since the aircraft entered service in the early 1980s. Derived from the 1960s vintage CH-53 family, the CH-53E incorporates a third engine to give it extra lifting power. It is now the standard heavy lift helicopter for the USMC. Its size generally restricts it to operations from amphibious landing craft and aircraft carriers but, since these ships form the backbone of any amphibious assault, there is no need for deployment aboard other ships. In addition to its lifting power, the CH-53E can be refuelled while in flight, giving it a much increased range. In 1990, two CH-53E Sea Stallions flew 856km (532 miles), refuelling mid-flight twice, to rescue US and foreign allies from the US Embassy in Mogadishu, Somalia. They saw further action in Bosnia, where two CH-53Es rescued downed US pilot Captain Scott O'Grady in 1995. The CH-53E is due to remain in service until the V-22 Osprey replaces it, and thus is undergoing a programme of upgrades and improvements to keep it airworthy until 2015.

SPECIFICATIONS

Manufacturer:	*Sikorsky Aircraft*
Mission:	*ship-based heavy-lift*
Length:	*30m (99ft)*
Height:	*8.5m (28ft)*
Rotor Diameter:	*24m (79ft)*
Crew:	*3/4*
Propulsion:	*3 x GE T64-416*
Horsepower:	*13,500 shaft horsepower*
Maximum Speed:	*315km/h (195mph)*
Cruise Speed:	*278km/h (172mph)*
Vertical Rate of Climb:	*750m/min (2500ft/min)*
Range:	*889km (550 miles)*
Weight:	*15,102kg (33,226lb)*
Date Deployed:	*1981*
Guns:	*2 x .50in machine guns*
Missiles:	*Sidewinder*
Systems:	*GPS, FLIR, chaff and flare dispenser*

CH-54A TARHE

The Sikorsky CH-54A Tarhe or Skycrane, with a crew of three, was designed for heavy internal or external lift of large bulk loads. It has a rear-facing pilot's seat to provide a clear view of the cargo. A hoist allows for the pickup and delivery of cargo without the need to land. One of the most interesting features of this helicopter, and most unusual in the world of aviation, is the utility of a vehicle stowed in the cargo area. A lightweight van (universal pod) could be attached to the fuselage for use as a mobile command post, maintenance and repair shop, or as a Mobile Army Surgical Hospital (MASH). Thus the Tarhe could be used as a rapid reaction mobile field hospital, able to medevac serious casualties, having given them first aid on the ground. A people pod was also designed to carry 45 combat-ready troops, and the Skycrane served with the 1st Cavalry Division in Vietnam. It was used in aircraft recovery operations when loads were too heavy for the CH-47 Chinook. It was also useful for offloading during ship-to-shore operations. On occasion the CH-54 could also be rigged to drop the 4536kg (10,000lb) daisy-cutter cratering bomb used to create landing zones in dense jungle. It was a truly useful helicopter, but was replaced by the less powerful but more flexible CH-47 Chinook. It now serves only in the US Army reserve forces.

SPECIFICATIONS

Manufacturer:	Sikorsky Aircraft
Mission:	heavy-lift transport
Length:	26.9m (88ft)
Height:	5.6m (19ft)
Rotor Diameter:	21.9m (72ft)
Crew:	3
Propulsion:	2 x Pratt & Whitney JFTD12-5A
Horsepower:	9350 shaft horsepower
Maximum Speed:	202km/h (126mph)
Cruise Speed:	169km/h (105mph)
Vertical Rate of Climb:	405m/min (1330ft/min)
Range:	370km (230 miles)
Weight:	8722kg (19,234lb)
Date Deployed:	1964
Guns:	none
Missiles:	none
Systems:	hoist, universal pod

SH-3 SEA KING

One of the world's most familiar helicopters, the SH-3 Sea King is a twin-engine, all-weather aircraft. The turbine-engined Sikorsky S-61 spawned a family of submarine hunters, airliners and rescue helicopters with offspring still serving around the world. Born as the Sea King anti-submarine helicopter for the US Navy, originally named HSS-2, the S-61 grew into different models and is now used by several countries. Although designed as an anti-submarine helicopter, it has been replaced in this role by newer, more capable aircraft. However, its utility has meant that it continues to serve in forces around the world, in some cases continuing in its original role as an ASW helicopter, but in most cases remodelled as a logistics or SAR aircraft. One of its most interesting design aspects is the boat-type hull, which allows it to remain bouyant for a time if forced to ditch into water. The basic H-3 design can easily be outfitted to perform many different roles, and it is this flexibility, along with its all-round ability, that has made it popular across the globe. The US and other technologically advanced countries have begun to replace the Sea King. However, the unhurried nature of defence development, procurement and delivery means that the helicopters will remain a familiar sight for many years to come.

SPECIFICATIONS

Manufacturer:	Sikorsky Aircraft
Mission:	logistical support
Length:	21.9m (73ft)
Height:	5.1m (17ft)
Rotor Diameter:	18.9m (62ft)
Crew:	4
Propulsion:	2 x GE T58-8F
Horsepower:	2850 shaft horsepower
Maximum Speed:	267km/h (166mph)
Cruise Speed:	217km/h (138mph)
Vertical Rate of Climb:	409m/min (1350ft/min)
Range:	1006km (625 miles)
Weight:	5339kg (11,865lb)
Date Deployed:	1961
Guns:	none
Missiles:	none
Systems:	GPS

HH-3E

Sikorsky's Jolly Green Giant, or HH-3E, is a heavy-lift helicopter employed by the US Army. It is used for recovery of personnel and aerospace hardware in support of global air and space operations. The twin-engined aircraft has also been used for combat and special operations. A modified version of the CH-3 transport helicopter, the HH-3E was developed for aircrew rescue missions deep in enemy-held territory during the Vietnam War. Many downed aircrews were rescued by Jolly Green Giants and their crews. This long-range machine has a hydraulically operated rear ramp for straight-inloading, and an ejectable sliding door on the right side at the front of the cabin. It has built-in equipment for the removal and replacement of all major components in remote areas. The Jolly Green Giant has an automatic flight-control system, instrumentation for all-weather operation, and Doppler navigation equipment. The HH-3E made the record books by making the first non-stop transatlantic flight by a helicopter in 1967, when two aircraft flew from New York City to the Paris air show. During that 6832km (4270-mile) flight, which took 30 hours and 46 minutes, each aircraft was aerially refuelled nine times. The Jolly Green Giant has also seen more recent action, flying 251 combat missions during Operation Desert Storm in 1991.

SPECIFICATIONS

Manufacturer:	*Sikorsky Aircraft*
Mission:	*combat recovery, special ops*
Length:	*22m (73ft)*
Height:	*5.5m (18ft)*
Rotor Diameter:	*18.8m (62ft)*
Crew:	*4*
Propulsion:	*2 x GE T58-5*
Horsepower:	*2900 shaft horsepower*
Maximum Speed:	*265km/h (165mph)*
Cruise Speed:	*243km/h (151mph)*
Vertical Rate of Climb:	*506m/min (1660ft/min)*
Range:	*965km (600 miles)*
Weight:	*5635kg (12,423lb)*
Date Deployed:	*1966*
Guns:	*none*
Missiles:	*none*
Systems:	*Doppler navigation equipment*

HH-60J JAYHAWK

The HH-60J Jayhawk is a medium-range recovery helicopter. It is used to perform SAR, law enforcement, military readiness and marine environmental protection missions. The USCG added 42 Jayhawks to its fleet of aircraft, replacing the Sikorsky HH-3F Pelican helicopters that the Coastguard has used for more than 20 years. The HH-60J is similar to the HH-3F in many ways, and the assigned missions are the same. However, the HH-60J has numerous upgrades including a state-of-the-art electronics package. The HH-60J is lighter, faster and the engines have more power. The Jayhawk can fly 480km (300 miles) offshore, remain on-scene for 45 minutes, recover six survivors, and return with spare fuel in reserve. The Jayhawk's cutting-edge radar, radio and navigation equipment enables the helicopter to carry out the USCG's SAR, law enforcement, military readiness and marine environmental protection missions efficiently and effectively. The Jayhawk uses the NAVSTAR Global Positioning System (GPS) as its primary long-range navigational aid. On board the Jayhawk, the Collins RCVR-3A radio simultaneously receives information from four of the system's 18 worldwide satellites and converts it into latitude fixes, pinpointing the helicopter's position.

SPECIFICATIONS

Manufacturer:	Sikorsky Aircraft
Mission:	SAR
Length:	13.6m (45ft)
Height:	5m (17ft)
Rotor Diameter:	16.4m (54ft)
Crew:	4
Propulsion:	2 x GE T700-401C
Horsepower:	3750 shaft horsepower
Maximum Speed:	333km/h (207mph)
Cruise Speed:	259km/h (161mph)
Vertical Rate of Climb:	not available
Range:	1296km (805 miles)
Weight:	6590kg (14,500lb)
Date Deployed:	1991
Guns:	none
Missiles:	none
Systems:	GPS, winch, Collins RCVR radio

HH-65A DOLPHIN

The USCG has added 96 short-range HH-65A helicopters to its fleet to replace the HH-52A Sikorsky Sea Guard. Although normally stationed onshore, the Dolphins can be carried on board medium- and high-endurance Coast Guard Cutters. They assist in the missions of SAR, law enforcement (including drug interdiction), polar ice-breaking, marine environmental protection (including pollution control) and military readiness. Helicopters stationed aboard icebreakers are the ships' eyes to find more navigable ice channels. They also airlift supplies to ships and to villages isolated by adverse weather. HH-65As are made of corrosion-resistant, composite materials. The shrouded tail rotor is unique to the Dolphin. Another special feature is its computerized flight management system that integrates state-of-the-art communications and navigation equipment. This system provides automatic flight control. At the pilot's direction, the system will bring the aircraft to a stable hover 15m (50ft) above a selected object. This is an important safety feature in darkness or in hazardous weather, which is quite common in USCG operations. The computer can select search patterns that can be flown automatically, freeing the pilot and co-pilot to concentrate on locating the object of the search.

SPECIFICATIONS

Manufacturer:	Aerospatiale/Textron Lycoming
Mission:	SAR, law enforcement
Length:	13.3m (44ft)
Height:	3.9m (13ft)
Rotor Diameter:	11.8m (39ft)
Crew:	4
Propulsion:	2 x Lycoming LTS
Horsepower:	1350 shaft horsepower
Maximum Speed:	296km/h (184mph)
Cruise Speed:	222km/h (138mph)
Vertical Rate of Climb:	not available
Range:	565km (353 miles)
Weight:	2750kg (6052lb)
Date Deployed:	1983
Guns:	none
Missiles:	none
Systems:	computerized flight system, GPS

K-1200 KMAX

Kaman's K-1200 KMAX helicopter is a unique design in the world of aviation. The main principle behind it is Kaman's intermeshing rotor technology with servo-flap control, which is exceptionally efficient at lifting heavy loads. The aircraft has counter-rotating main rotors and no tail rotor, which means all engine power goes directly to the main rotors for the highest lifting capacity of any rotor configuration. The aircraft's rugged construction allows it to fly repetitive, short operational cycles eight to 10 hours a day. This has interested a number of parties, which are keen to utilize the KMAX's lifting power. These potential purchasers range from lumber companies to oil firms and, of course, the military. The KMAX has demonstrated successfully its capability to perform vertical supply replenishment of US Navy ships at sea. However, the USMC envisages a pilotless KMAX fulfilling a new tactical concept for re-supplying troops on land from fast-moving ships at sea. The future of the KMAX is clearly unmanned. Yet, until this becomes a viable option, the KMAX will continue to be flown by one pilot. When the technology becomes viable for the KMAX to be fully automated, it could herald a revolution in the way in which the USMC conducts its operations.

SPECIFICATIONS

Manufacturer:	*Kaman Aerospace*
Mission:	*external-lift transport*
Length:	*15.9m (52ft)*
Height:	*4.1m (13ft)*
Rotor Diameter:	*2x 14.7m (48ft)*
Crew:	*1*
Propulsion:	*1 x Allied Signal T-5317A-1*
Horsepower:	*1500 shaft horsepower*
Maximum Speed:	*185km/h (115mph)*
Cruise Speed:	*165km/h (102mph)*
Vertical Rate of Climb:	*762m/min (2500ft/min)*
Range:	*460km (285 miles)*
Weight:	*2313kg (5100lb)*
Date Deployed:	*1994*
Guns:	*none*
Missiles:	*none*
Systems:	*not available*

MH-47E SOA CHINOOK

The MH-47E Special Operations Aircraft (SOA) is a derivative of the Boeing CH-47 Chinook. Included with other adaptations is a significantly increased fuel capacity with modified main and auxiliary fuel tanks. The aircraft's integrated avionics suites and multi-mode radars have also been updated. It is intended to provide adverse-weather infiltration/extraction and support to US armed forces, country teams, other agencies and special activities. The CH-47D Chinook has been specially modified to perform special operations missions, and has been tested in combat. It provides long-range penetration, medium-assault helicopter support to special operations. During Operation Desert Storm in 1991, the MH-47E's predecessor, the CH-47, conducted infiltration and extraction of special forces troops and downed pilots. The distinctive twin-rotor design of the MH-47E makes it one of the most easily recognizable helicopters in the world. In the case of the special forces Chinook it is also one of the most technologically advanced. Capable of flying low level over any terrain, in any conditions, the MH-47E has become a firm favourite with special forces the world over, and is used extensively by the US Delta Force and the British SAS. The Chinook is equipped with a suite of countermeasure systems selected by the customer country.

SPECIFICATIONS

Manufacturer:	The Boeing Company
Mission:	covert infiltration of special forces
Length:	15.6m (51ft)
Height:	5.8m (19ft)
Rotor Diameter:	2 x 18.3m (60ft)
Crew:	3
Propulsion:	2 x Textron Lycoming T55-L-712
Horsepower:	7500 shaft horsepower
Maximum Speed:	269km/h (167mph)
Cruise Speed:	265km/h (165mph)
Vertical Rate of Climb:	561m/min (1841ft/min)
Range:	1136km (705 miles)
Weight:	12,210kg (27,000lb)
Date Deployed:	1993
Guns:	6 x M-60 machine guns
Missiles:	none
Systems:	FLIR, terrain radar, flare/chaff

MH-53J PAVE LOW III

Low-level, long-range, undetected penetration into denied areas, day or night, in adverse weather conditions is the mission of the MH-53J Pave Low IIIE helicopter. It specializes in the infiltration, extraction and re-supply of special operations forces. The Pave Low III heavy-lift helicopter is one of the largest and most powerful in the US Air Force (USAF) inventory, and one of the most technologically advanced helicopters in the world. Its terrain-following, terrain-avoidance radar and FLIR sensor, along with a projected map display, enable the crew to follow terrain contours and avoid obstacles, making low-level penetration possible. The helicopter is equipped with armour plating, and a combination of three 7.62mm miniguns or .50-calibre machine guns. It can transport 38 troops and has an external cargo hook with a 9000kg (20,000lb) capacity. Derived from the Sikorsky HH-3E Jolly Green Giant, its modifications include the aforementioned FLIR, GPS, Doppler navigation systems, an on-board computer and integrated avionics to enable precise navigation to and from target areas. The MH-53J Pave Low saw extensive action during Operation Desert Storm, and has been in continual use as a special operations infiltration/extraction helicopter.

SPECIFICATIONS

Manufacturer:	Sikorsky Aircraft
Mission:	covert infiltration/extraction
Length:	28m (92ft)
Height:	7.6m (25ft)
Rotor Diameter:	21.9m (72ft)
Crew:	6
Propulsion:	2 x GE T64-416
Horsepower:	8500 shaft horsepower
Maximum Speed:	320km/h (199mph)
Cruise Speed:	264km/h (165mph)
Vertical Rate of Climb:	762m/min (2500ft/min)
Range:	1014km (630 miles)
Weight:	16,561kg (36,435lb)
Date Deployed:	1981
Guns:	3 x 7.62mm miniguns
Missiles:	none
Systems:	GPS, FLIR, terrain-following radar

MH-60G PAVE HAWK

The MH-60G Pave Hawk is a modern, medium-lift, special operations helicopter for missions requiring medium- to long-range infiltration, extraction and re-supply of special operations forces on land or sea. It is equipped with FLIR to enable its crew to follow more easily terrain contours and avoid obstacles at night. The MH-60G's primary wartime missions are special operations forces support in day, night or marginal weather conditions. Other missions include combat SAR. As a highly modified variant of the UH-60A Black Hawk, the MH-60G offers increased capability in range (endurance), navigation, communications and defensive systems. It can be used to provide a full range of special air warfare activities including special operations, psychological operations and civil affairs. The MH-60G can be deployed by airlift or sealift, and it can also be self-deployed. The preferred option is airlift using a C-5 Galaxy fixed-wing aircraft, and is essential if rapid deployment is required. A Galaxy can transport a maximum of five MH-60Gs. The aircraft can be broken down for shipment in less than one hour and off-loaded and rebuilt at the location in less than two hours. The optimum deployment package is four MH-60Gs via a C-5.

SPECIFICATIONS

Manufacturer:	Sikorsky Aircraft
Mission:	special operations
Length:	13.6m (45ft)
Height:	5m (17ft)
Rotor Diameter:	16.4m (54ft)
Crew:	4
Propulsion:	2 x GE T700-701C
Horsepower:	3000 shaft horsepower
Maximum Speed:	294km/h (184mph)
Cruise Speed:	270km/h (171mph)
Vertical Rate of Climb:	not available
Range:	833km (517 miles)
Weight:	6590kg (14,500lb)
Date Deployed:	1994
Guns:	1 x 7.62mm M-60 machine gun
Missiles:	none
Systems:	GPS, PNVG, terrain-following radar

MH-68A ENFORCER

A specially built version of the commercial Agusta A109 Power, the MH-68A Enforcer is in service with the USCG. It made its first operational flight in 2000. The Coastguard has recently deployed a number of these aircraft to be used primarily in its anti-drug operations. They operate from the flight-deck of the USCG's medium-endurance cutters as part of its counter-narcotics mission. It has become necessary for USCG helicopters to be armed because of the increased sophistication of the drug cartels, not to mention their increased willingness to take on US ships and aircraft. The MH-68 is a particularly well-equipped machine, with a rescue hoist, emergency floats, .50-calibre sniper rifle with laser sight, M-240 machine gun, PNVG, FLIR, Light Eye and NightSun searchlight. Avionics include a fully integrated avionics suite, Head-Up Display (HUD) and GPS moving map. It has already seen a great deal of action and scored a remarkable number of successes. Use of the helicopter by the USCG allows the Coastuard to bring down precise fire on to the target vessel in order to disable it. This strategy has contributed greatly to the improvement in the USCG's anti-drugs success rate.

SPECIFICATIONS

Manufacturer:	Agusta
Mission:	coast guard, law enforcement
Length:	13.5m (43ft)
Height:	3.3m (10ft)
Rotor Diameter:	11m (36ft)
Crew:	3
Propulsion:	2 x P & W Canada PW206C
Horsepower:	800 shaft horsepower
Maximum Speed:	305km/h (190mph)
Cruise Speed:	265km/h (165mph)
Vertical Rate of Climb:	not available
Range:	565km (353 miles)
Weight:	1415kg (3113lb)
Date Deployed:	2000
Guns:	1 x .50in rifle, M-240 machine gun
Missiles:	none
Systems:	GPS, FLIR, PNVG, searchlight, hoist

OH-58D KIOWA

Bell's OH-58D Kiowa Warrior is an aircraft that was born not from conceptual ideas but from the need to counter the threat posed by gunboats to vital shipping in the Persian Gulf during 1987. Developed from the successful OH-58 series of light helicopters, the Kiowa Warrior is an armed reconnaissance aircraft carrying a crew of two. It was conceived and developed in less than 100 days and was so successful in deterring gunboat activity that the US Army was immediately convinced of its capabilities and placed an order for all existing OH-58 Kiowas to be upgraded. The current version will eventually be replaced by the Comanche, but until then the OH-58D is a vital component of the US Army's aerial fighting force. The machine is equipped with one .50in heavy machine gun and can carry FFAR rockets, Stinger and Hellfire missiles. The primary mission of the Kiowa Warrior is armed reconnaissance in air cavalry and light attack companies. In addition, the Kiowa Warrior may be called upon to participate in other missions or tasks such as joint air attack operations, air combat, limited attack operation or artillery target designation. The distinctive mast-mounted sight, which incorporates a thermal imaging system, a laser range finder, a television sensor and a boresight system, is one of the key elements of the Kiowa Warrior.

SPECIFICATIONS

Manufacturer:	Bell Helicopter Textron
Mission:	armed reconnaissance
Length:	12.5m (41ft)
Height:	4m (13ft)
Rotor Diameter:	10.7m (35ft)
Crew:	2
Propulsion:	1 x T703-AD-700
Horsepower:	650 shaft horsepower
Maximum Speed:	237km/h (147mph)
Cruise Speed:	166km/h (100mph)
Vertical Rate of Climb:	152m/min (500ft/min)
Range:	480km (300 miles)
Weight:	2040kg (4500lb)
Date Deployed:	1991
Guns:	1 x 50in heavy machine gun
Missiles:	FFAR, Stinger, Hellfire
Systems:	thermal imaging, rangefinder

OH-6A CAYUSE

The Boeing OH-6A was designed for use as a military scout during the Vietnam War to meet the US Army's need for an extremely manoeuvrable light-observation helicopter. The Hughes OH-6A Cayuse was quite effective when teamed with the AH-1G Cobra attack helicopter. The OH-6A Loach would find targets by flying low, "trolling" for fire, and lead in a Cobra, or Snake, to attack. The OH-6A can be armed with the M-27 armament subsystem, the M-134 six-barrel 7.62mm "minigun" or the M-129 40mm grenade launcher on the XM8 armament subsystem. Two special operations versions of the OH-6A are the Little Bird AH-6C armed variant, and the MH-6B transport/utility version, which can carry up to six personnel for quick insertion and extraction missions. A previous version, the EH-6B, was used for command, control and radio relay. The MH-6 Little Bird is the only light-assault helicopter in the army inventory. It provides assault-helicopter support to special operations forces, and can be armed with a combination of guns and FFAR. It has an un-refuelled range of 463km (250 nautical miles). The AH-6 Little Bird Gun, a light-attack version of the helicopter, has been tested and proven in combat when armed with guns, Hellfire missiles and 2.75in FFAR rockets.

SPECIFICATIONS

Manufacturer:	*The Boeing Company*
Mission:	*armed reconnaissance*
Length:	*7.6m (25ft)*
Height:	*2.6m (8ft)*
Rotor Diameter:	*8m (26ft)*
Crew:	*2*
Propulsion:	*1 x Allison T63*
Horsepower:	*317 shaft horsepower*
Maximum Speed:	*241km/h (149mph)*
Cruise Speed:	*221km/h (137mph)*
Vertical Rate of Climb:	*504m/min (1654ft/min)*
Range:	*485km (301 miles)*
Weight:	*896kg (1975lb)*
Date Deployed:	*1962*
Guns:	*1 x 7.62mm machine gun*
Missiles:	*grenade launcher, FFAR*
Systems:	*GPS, FLIR. chaff/flare dispenser*

RAH-66 COMANCHE

The RAH-66 Comanche is believed to represent the future of the US aerial reconnaissance and light attack helicopter force, and is expected to be a key element in the strategic vision of achieving dominant battlespace awareness. Its primary role will be to seek out enemy forces and designate targets for the AH-64 Apache attack helicopter. This can take place at night, in adverse weather and on obscured battlefields, using advanced infrared sensors. To succeed in this role, the Comanche has been designed with speed and stealth in mind. Coupled with the next generation of sophisticated sensors and weapons systems, this makes it a truly formidable aircraft. The Comanche incorporates more low-observable stealth features than any aircraft in US Army history, with the radar cross-section (RCS) being less than that of a Hellfire missile. To reduce RCS, weapons can be carried internally, the gun can be rotated aft and stowed within a fairing behind the turret when not in use, and the landing gear is fully retractable. In short, the Comanche has no peers. Military budgets permitting, when it is officially brought into service in 2006, the US Army will have at its disposal a vastly capable, sophisticated and versatile helicopter to provide unparalleled target detection and acquisition.

SPECIFICATIONS

Manufacturer:	*Boeing Sikorsky*
Mission:	*reconnaissance, attack*
Length:	*12.7m (42ft)*
Height:	*3.3m (11ft)*
Rotor Diameter:	*11.8m (39ft)*
Crew:	*2*
Propulsion:	*2 x T800-LHTEC-801*
Horsepower:	*3126 shaft horsepower*
Maximum Speed:	*330 km/h (206mph)*
Cruise Speed:	*310 km/h (193mph)*
Vertical Rate of Climb:	*530m/min (1750ft/min)*
Range:	*480km (300 miles)*
Weight:	*3950kg (8690lb)*
Date Deployed:	*2006*
Guns:	*1 x XM301 20mm auto-cannon*
Missiles:	*Hellfire, Stinger, 70mm FFAR*
Systems:	*GPS, FLIR*

S-92 HELIBUS

Sikorsky's S-92 Helibus is based on the proven US Army UH-60 Black Hawk and US Navy SH-60 Seahawk helicopters. The manufacturer is actively marketing the S-92 for military requirements in Canada, Portugal and Scandinavia. The Helibus is designed to answer the needs of users requiring greater payload and range characteristics than those provided by the Black Hawk. Improvements include more powerful engines, seating capacity for 22 troops in the stretched cabin, and a rear loading ramp. It has been designed to compete directly against Europe's EH 101 Merlin, the NH-90 and a variety of Eurocopter-built medium-utility aircraft. The S-92 is a truly multinational effort, with manufacturers from many countries contributing to the project. These include Mitsubishi Heavy Industries of Japan (main cabin), Jingdezhen Helicopter Group of China (vertical tail surfaces), Gamesa of Spain (aft transmission tailcone and "strongback" composite structure), Aerospace Industrial Development Corporation of Taiwan (flight deck and other parts) and Embraer of Brazil (sponsons, fuel cells and gauging systems). Despite an initial lack of firm orders, Sikorsky remains confident that the S-92 will be drafted into service with a number of armed forces to replace their current fleets.

SPECIFICATIONS

Manufacturer:	Sikorsky Aircraft
Mission:	medium utility
Length:	17.3m (57ft)
Height:	6.4m (21ft)
Rotor Diameter:	17.7m (58ft)
Crew:	3
Propulsion:	2 x CT7-8
Horsepower:	4800 shaft horsepower
Maximum Speed:	280km/h (175mph)
Cruise Speed:	252km/h (157mph)
Vertical Rate of Climb:	not available
Range:	880km (550 miles)
Weight:	7030kg (15,500lb)
Date Deployed:	2001
Guns:	2 x 7.62mm machine guns
Missiles:	none
Systems:	GPS, PNVG

SH-60B SEAHAWK

The Sikorsky-built SH-60B Seahawk is the US Navy version of the US Army's highly effective UH-60 Black Hawk helicopter. It can fulfil many different roles, ranging from ASW, medevac and SAR. However, this particular aircraft is used primarily as an ASW platform, based onboard US Navy frigates, destroyers and cruisers. Introduced during the 1980s, the SH-60 Seahawk has become the standard aircraft onboard a great many of the US Navy's warships and has seen service throughout the world. Designed and built during the height of the Cold War with the former USSR, it was originally tasked to hunt Soviet submarines, although its original remit has now been expanded to take on other roles. The Seahawk, with its crew of three, can lower its sonobuoy, acoustic equipment or MAD more than 450m (1500ft) into the ocean and then detect or track enemy submarines. If configured to do so, the SH-60 can use Mk 50 torpedoes to attack any targets to a range of around 1500m (5000ft). In addition to its own armament and systems, the SH-60 has a datalink connected to its parent ship through which it can send and receive information on targets in the area of operation. It can thereby increase greatly the efficiency of the US Navy's various fleets in locating and neutralizing any subsea threats.

SPECIFICATIONS

Manufacturer:	Sikorsky Aircraft
Mission:	ASW
Length:	15.3m (50ft)
Height:	3.8m (13ft)
Rotor Diameter:	16.4m (54ft)
Crew:	3
Propulsion:	2 x GE T700-701C
Horsepower:	3400 shaft horsepower
Maximum Speed:	296km/h (184mph)
Cruise Speed:	250km/h (155mph)
Vertical Rate of Climb:	545m/min (1800ft/min)
Range:	833km (518 miles)
Weight:	6191kg (13,650lb)
Date Deployed:	1983
Guns:	1 x 7.62mm M-60 machine gun
Missiles:	Mk 50 torpedoes, Penguin AGM
Systems:	GPS, LAMPS, RAST, sonobuoy

TH-67 CREEK

Bell Helicopter Textron has built the US Army's TH-67 New Training Helicopter (NTH), developed from the hugely successful Bell 206 JetRanger. The aircraft's function is to replace existing UH-1H Hueys being used to train Initial Entry Rotary Wing (IERW) students. These Hueys have been the army's interim trainer since the 1988 retirement of the TH-55 Osage. The TH-67 Creek is a state-of-the-art helicopter and the aircraft of choice for a new generation of army aviators. In the tactical portion of pilot training, the OH-58 Kiowa is still the helicopter used given its war-configured characteristics. But, for IERW flight instruction, the new TH-67 is the ideal machine. For a new Aviation Lieutenant, flight school means the successful completion of Aviation Officer Basic Course (AVOBC) Phase I, AVOBC Phase II IERW Qualification, AVOBC Phase III, and an Advanced Aircraft Qualification Course (AAQC). Every two weeks, an IERW class starts and the TH-67 Creek's primary mission begins. The first 20 weeks of training involve learning the basics of helicopter flight and instruments in the TH-67. At the end of primary flight and instruments, most officers will move on to Basic Combat Skills (BCS) and PNVG in the Bell-designed OH-58C Kiowa.

SPECIFICATIONS

Manufacturer:	*Bell Helicopter Textron*
Mission:	*training*
Length:	*9.5m (31ft)*
Height:	*2.9m (10ft)*
Rotor Diameter:	*10.2m (34ft)*
Crew:	*1*
Propulsion:	*1 x Alison 250-C20J*
Horsepower:	*420 shaft horsepower*
Maximum Speed:	*225km/h (140mph)*
Cruise Speed:	*216km/h (135mph)*
Vertical Rate of Climb:	*384m/min (1267ft/min)*
Range:	*748km (467 miles)*
Weight:	*742kg (1632lb)*
Date Deployed:	*2001*
Guns:	*none*
Missiles:	*none*
Systems:	*basic flight systems*

UH-1H HUEY

A legend, the remarkable Bell UH-1 Iroquois (Huey) is the most famous helicopter in the world, linked forever with images of the Vietnam War. It has been the quintessential all-purpose military helicopter for more than three decades. It has been used by all four US services and international forces in missions ranging from mountain rescue to troop transport, and from anti-armour to ASW. The Huey got its distinctive nickname from its original US Army designation, the HU-1. It was later redesignated UH-1, under a tri-service agreement. The UH-1 Iroquois is used for command and control, medical evacuation, and to transport personnel, equipment and supplies. The latest models are the UH-1H and the UH-1V. Initially procured in 1959, the Huey is the senior member of the army's helicopter fleet. The last production aircraft was delivered in 1976. More than 9000 were produced in 20 years, evolving through 13 models. Considered to be the most widely used helicopter in the world, the Huey is flown by about 40 countries. In 1995 the army's UH-1 residual fleet was projected to be approximately 1000 aircraft. Though the technology in the UH-1 has been largely made redundant by newer aircraft, the US armed forces still envisage keeping 700 aircraft in service until 2015.

SPECIFICATIONS

Manufacturer:	*Bell Helicopter Textron*
Mission:	*multi-role transport*
Length:	*12.8m (42ft)*
Height:	*4.4m (14ft)*
Rotor Diameter:	*14.6m (48ft)*
Crew:	*3*
Propulsion:	*1 x Lycoming T53-L13B*
Horsepower:	*1100 shaft horsepower*
Maximum Speed:	*204km/h (127mph)*
Cruise Speed:	*185km/h (115mph)*
Vertical Rate of Climb:	*485m/min (1600ft/min)*
Range:	*370km (231 miles)*
Weight:	*2600kg (5800lb)*
Date Deployed:	*1985*
Guns:	*2 x 7.62mm M-60 machine guns*
Missiles:	*none*
Systems:	*PNVG, rescue winch, searchlight*

UH-1N HUEY

One successful variant of the renowned Huey is the UH-1N light-lift utility helicopter, used by the US Air Force Space Command (USAFSC) missile wings and groups. Its primary roles include airlift of emergency security and disaster response forces, security surveillance of off-base nuclear weapons movements, space shuttle landing support and SAR operations. The USMC and US Army both use the UH-1N because of the speed with which it can be reconfigured for varying roles, but the USAF variant is used almost exclusively by the USAFSC. It is capable of night flight, and can seat up to 13 people. The usual number of crew is two, the pilot and his co-pilot, but in hoist, water and navigational operations the crew is three, with a flight engineer added. Synonymous with the popular image of the Vietnam War, the Huey served with great distinction in all of the US armed forces during the lengthy conflict, and its success cemented hundreds of sales for the manufacturer Bell (more than 5000 served in Southeast Asia in the 1960s). Though originally designed and built in the late 1950s, the Huey still finds itself on the battlefield in its various guises, almost half a century after its conception. Having been in service for almost 50 years, the UH-1N will continue to serve well into the future such is the durability and flexibility of its classic design.

SPECIFICATIONS

Manufacturer:	Bell Helicopter Textron
Mission:	multi-role transport
Length:	12.8m (42ft)
Height:	4.4m (14ft)
Rotor Diameter:	14.6m (48ft)
Crew:	3
Propulsion:	1 x Lycoming T53-L13B
Horsepower:	1100 shaft horsepower
Maximum Speed:	204km/h (127mph)
Cruise Speed:	185km/h (115mph)
Vertical Rate of Climb:	485m/min (1600ft/min)
Range:	370km (231 miles)
Weight:	2600kg (5800lb)
Date Deployed:	1983
Guns:	none
Missiles:	none
Systems:	GPS, winch

UH-60L BLACK HAWK

The UH-60L Black Hawk is one of the US Army's most recognizable and widely used aircraft. Brought into service towards the end of the 1970s, it is designed as a multi-purpose utility helicopter. In this capacity it is able to transport up to 11 fully armed troops, one 105mm howitzer or many other types of cargo up to a weight of 10,000kg (22,000lb). The Black Hawk has performed admirably in a variety of missions, including air assault, air cavalry and aeromedical evacuations. In addition, modified Black Hawks operate as command and control, electronic warfare and special operations platforms. The UH-60L variant is the workhorse of the US Army, and it has been involved in every operation where US soldiers have been needed. Introduced in 1989, the UH-60L is an improvement on the UH-60A, expanding the lifetime of the aircraft and making it more capable. It is able to utilize the External Supplies Support System (ESSS) to tailor the aircraft to any given mission, be it in an attack support role with Hellfire missiles or as an aerial minelayer, or even in a reconnaissance capacity. It is an extremely reliable and durable aircraft, and as such has become popular with armed forces the world over. The airframe has lent itself to all manner of roles, including the naval Seahawk version.

SPECIFICATIONS

Manufacturer:	Sikorsky Aircraft
Mission:	multi-mission utility
Length:	19.5m (64ft)
Height:	4.8m (16ft)
Rotor Diameter:	16.5m (53ft)
Crew:	3
Propulsion:	2 x GE T700-701C
Horsepower:	3400 shaft horsepower
Maximum Speed:	296km/h (184mph)
Cruise Speed:	257km/h (160mph)
Vertical Rate of Climb:	472m/min (1550 ft/min)
Range:	584km (363 miles)
Weight:	5224kg (11,516lb)
Date Deployed:	1989
Guns:	2 x 7.62mm M-60 machine guns
Missiles:	Hellfire, FFAR
Systems:	ESSS

V-22 OSPREY

B oeing's revolutionary V-22 Osprey is a utility transport helicopter with a difference, combining the benefits of rotary- and fixed-wing flight. While the traditional helicopter is suitable for many conditions, it lacks the speed or range of traditional airplanes, and the one successful vertical take-off and landing (VTOL) fixed-wing jet aircraft, the Harrier, is vastly expensive to build and maintain. The V-22 Osprey appears to have solved the problem. Designed to take full advantage of a helicopter's versatility and VTOL capability, plus the fixed-wing aircraft's speed and range, the V-22 Osprey will replace the medium-lift helicopters in all of the US armed services. Despite many teething troubles and setbacks, the Osprey is gradually being brought into service and is proving itself to be highly effective. It works by rotating its propellers to a vertical position in order to take off, and then tilts them to a horizontal position for normal flight. It can then tilt the rotors back to a vertical position to land. This allows it to operate from the deck of a ship, in a confined area or on damaged runways in war-torn areas of the world. A similar machine, the BA609 tilt-rotor aircraft, is currently on trial with the USCG. All of the key US helicopter operators look set to take advantage of tilt-rotor technology.

SPECIFICATIONS

Manufacturer:	*The Boeing Company*
Mission:	*utility transport*
Length:	*17.3m (57ft)*
Height:	*6.7m (22ft)*
Rotor Diameter:	*2 x 11.6m (38ft)*
Crew:	*3*
Propulsion:	*2 x Allison T406-AD-400*
Horsepower:	*12,300 shaft horsepower*
Maximum Speed:	*630km/h (390mph)*
Cruise Speed:	*503km/h (313mph)*
Vertical Rate of Climb:	*332m/min (1090ft/min)*
Range:	*954km (515 miles)*
Weight:	*15,032kg (33,140lb)*
Date Deployed:	*2001*
Guns:	*2 x .50in machine guns*
Missiles:	*none*
Systems:	*VTOL Tiltrotor, electronic warfare*

INDEX